SELF·DEVELOPMENT FOR SUCCESS

Business writing

D1530036

Acknowledgments

The following have contributed to the preparation of this book or to the development of

the approaches taken in it:

Renee Gillies

Institute of Personnel and Development

Jim Kelly

Bridie Pritchard

Graham Scrivener, sales and marketing director at

  In Tuition Computer Training

Alan Shaw

Business writing

THE ESSENTIAL GUIDE TO THINKING AND WORKING SMARTER

Midge Gillies

AMERICAN MANAGEMENT ASSOCIATION

AMACOM
American Management Association
New York • Atlanta • Boston • Chicago • Kansas City
San Francisco • Washington, D. C.
Brussels • Mexico City • Tokyo • Toronto

A Marshall Edition
Conceived, edited, and designed by
Marshall Editions Ltd.
The Orangery, 161 New Bond Street
London W1Y 9PA

This book is available at a special discount when ordered in bulk quantities. For information, contact Special Sales Department, AMACOM, an imprint of AMA Publications, a division of American Management Association,1601 Broadway, New York, NY 10019.

This publication is designed to provide accurate and authoritative information in regard to the subject matter covered. It is sold with the understanding that the publisher is not engaged in rendering legal, accounting, or other professional service. If legal advice or other expert assistance is required, the services of a competent professional person should be sought.

Library of Congress Cataloging-in-Publication Data
Gillies, Midge, 1962-
    Business Writing / Midge Gillies.
        p. cm.
    Includes bibliographical references and index.
    ISBN: 0-8144-7068-8
    1. Business Writing I. Title

HF5718.3 .G55 2000
808.06665--dc21   99-053920
                    CIP

Printing number

10 9 8 7 6 5 4 3 2 1

Series Consultant Editor Chris Roebuck
Project Editor Theresa Reynolds
Design Axis Design
Art Director Dave Goodman
Managing Art Editor Patrick Carpenter
Managing Editor Conor Kilgallon
Editorial Assistant Dan Green
Editorial Coordinator Ros Highstead
Production Angela Kew

Cover photography The Stock Market

Originated in Italy by Articolor
Printed and bound in Portugal by Printer Portuguesa

Contents

1

Business writing matters
Identify your strengths
Make yourself understood
Know when to write

Why do you write at work?
Are you wasting words?
What are you trying to say?

Why effective business writing is important

In today's fast-moving business world it is easy to overlook the importance of the written word. When startling new ideas emerge from frenetic brainstorming sessions, products are bought and sold over the Internet and deals are done by video-conferences and mobile phones, it can be difficult to see why anybody would need a piece of paper with words on it.

But it is precisely because the world of business moves so fast that clear and effective writing is more important than ever before. The new idea can only become reality when it is written down and passed on to the people who will determine whether it is viable. The Internet may be able to link millions of people around the world, but its success still relies on its users' ability to communicate effectively with each other in writing. A deal is only really "done" when everyone involved has drawn up a document to ensure that they are all agreeing to the same thing.

How writing smooths the way

Rather than slowing down a business transaction, a written communication ensures that there are no misunderstandings to hold up the process. Writing can slow things down, however, if it is poorly worded. This is true for any form of business writing.

Your writing reflects you

You may be excellent at talking and listening to people or at giving presentations, but your written skills are just as important. They may even be more important because a written document could lie around on someone's desk or in a filing cabinet for weeks or months as a record of your thoughts and abilities.

If the document is muddled and poorly thought out, you may be viewed in a similar way. If it is easy to follow and helps your organization to carry out a project quickly and efficiently, it will leave an impression about your skills that could prove as lasting as the document itself.

HOW WRITING HELPS YOU

Take a minute to consider how often you rely on written communication to make sure the day runs smoothly. The list might include the instructions on a carton that tell you how to open it without spilling milk on your work clothes, the newspaper that explains the latest development in your industry and the detour notice that helps you to avoid the road crews on the way to the office – and that's before you start work.

POOR WRITING SKILLS AFFECT EVERY PART OF OUR LIVES

Think back over the last week or so to see how often you have been misled or confused by a poor piece of writing.

■ Perhaps you were upset by an e-mail because the sender's tone of voice seemed abusive or rude?
■ Has a letter from a government official or a lawyer left you baffled by its long-winded sentences and use of old-fashioned terms?
■ Did you waste hours trying to understand the instructions on a new piece of equipment?
■ Was a note left by a colleague so confusing that it became virtually meaningless?
■ Did a memo fail to provide relevant times and dates?
■ Was a customer upset when his or her letter went unanswered because it was addressed to a department rather than a person?

What was the consequence of the poor communication in each case?
■ Perhaps your relationship with a colleague is a lot cooler after their abusive e-mail.
■ Were you put off dealing with an official letter because you couldn't understand it?
■ Were you reluctant to buy another product from a manufacturer because the instructions are so difficult to follow?
■ Is a colleague upset with you because you ignored a note?
■ Perhaps several people missed a meeting because a memo failed to say when it was due to start.
■ Maybe a customer wrote to a local newspaper complaining about service because you didn't respond to the initial complaint?

Contrasting case studies

- **How often does something you write raise more questions than it answers?**
- **Do you use writing as a way of avoiding confrontation?**
- **Have you ever heard a colleague making a joke of something you've written that wasn't meant to be funny?**

You probably haven't given much thought to when and how you use the written word – it's just something you do. But, as these two case studies show, effective writing can have a big impact on whether you have a good day or a bad day. It can boost productivity and improve relationships with colleagues. And it's just as important out of the office, too.

Your attitude may not be as extreme as either Roger's or Jim's, but you'll probably recognize a few of their habits.

Roger's attitude to writing

Just before he leaves the house in the morning, with a half-eaten piece of toast in one hand, Roger scribbles a note to his wife reminding her that he is playing squash after work that evening. He leaves it on the refridgerator door; and, as he jumps in the car he makes a mental note to call her later in case she doesn't spot the message, or can't read it.

At work he has to answer five e-mails asking about a message he sent out yesterday. As they are slightly different questions he has to send five individual replies.

Roger's mail contains a letter from a customer who hasn't understood some of the technical terms he used in a recent letter. Roger calls to explain what he meant. While he's on the phone, his boss arrives to discuss something with him but, because Roger has scribbled the wrong time in his planner, he isn't prepared.

Instead of writing up his notes immediately after the meeting, Roger has to tackle a report he's been putting off for weeks and which is due today. It's too short, so he adds a little air with some technical jargon, does a quick spell check, and asks his secretary to print and circulate it.

The afternoon is taken up with meetings – which is what Roger really enjoys – but he forgets to call his wife who becomes worried when he doesn't come home at the normal time.

KEY POINTS

- Has to follow up written note to wife with phone call
- Spends time having to clarify badly written messages
- Fails to provide written reference for technical information
- Puts off writing minutes, which will make it more difficult
- Keeps planner inefficiently
- Rushes writing a report and then fails to check it properly
- Creates bad impression by filling report with jargon

Jim's attitude to writing

A schedule of squash games is pinned to the noticeboard in Jim's kitchen, so he doesn't need to remind his wife that he will be late home.

He has four e-mails confirming that a message was received and understood, one from a friend, and one requesting information about a new product. Jim just has time to reply to the request before a meeting. He resists the temptation to answer his friend's e-mail, but does send an e-mail to a peer about a "difficult" subject rather than confront him in person.

After the meeting Jim makes a few quick notes that he will write up at the end of the day. He looks at the report he's been working on and makes the changes to it suggested by a manager, does a spell check, and then takes a print-out to read over lunch.

When a supplier calls to say he doesn't understand technical terms in a letter from the company Jim sends a written explanation the supplier can refer to in the future.

As he knows he'll be in meetings all afternoon, Jim sends an e-mail to his friend saying he'll call him later. He leaves an entry on the office calendar saying where the meetings are and how long they will last. Next to one he adds, "Do not disturb unless urgent".

Conclusion

Both Roger and Jim could improve their approach to writing. Roger doesn't see the importance of writing and wastes time as a result, following up with calls and responding to requests for clarification. The bad impression he creates is more lasting than his consistently good performance at work.

Jim takes written communications more seriously, providing clear written information. He checks his report thoroughly and has someone else read it. But he is not a good judge of when a written message is appropriate, and sometimes hides behind a written communication.

KEY POINTS

- Written schedule lets wife know in advance when he will be late
- Sends clear written messages, so no additional time is wasted on clarification
- Keeps planner efficiently, including relative importance of meetings, as well as time, place, and likely duration
- Makes notes for minutes immediately after meeting
- Provides technical information in written form
- Starts writing report well in advance to leave time for adequate checking
- Gets a co-worker to read report for additional feedback before printing and distributing

How good are your writing skills?

Many of us have a fear of writing. But confronting an anxiety usually helps to reduce its power over us. If we practice something regularly, it becomes easier. If you're honest about answering the following questions, you should have a better idea of your own attitude to writing.

TO WRITE OR NOT TO WRITE?

TIME TO TALK

You need to recognize the situations when writing would waste time or would slow things down. It is better to talk if:

- Writing would be a way to avoid a difficult situation: if you dislike phoning or meeting someone, for example, you may take refuge in writing.
- The message is personal and a written record could cause embarrassment later; – for example, if you need to confront a team member for dressing inappropriately.
- You want an instant reaction.
- Something needs to be discussed.
- You want to give your audience the chance to ask questions on the spot.

TIME TO WRITE

Managers think they can make up for any misunderstanding by addressing their audience face to face. However, write if:

- You need to clarify your thoughts and make sure you are sending out the same message to everyone.
- You are communicating information, such as the schedule for a project, where people need a written record rather than having to rely on their memory of what you said.
- The message is complicated or technical, so people will need time to digest it.
- You want your message to carry more weight or authority.

Scoring Method

Questions: 1, 2, 3, 4, 5.

1 = Usually
2 = Sometimes
3 = Seldom

Questions: 6, 7, 8, 9, 10.

1 = Seldom
2 = Sometimes
3 = Usually

	Statement	Score
1	I only put something in writing if I'm forced to by my boss.	
2	I leave a piece of writing to the very last moment.	
3	I like to use long words and sentences; they make my writing seem more important.	
4	I often feel vague about the reason why I'm writing something.	
5	I don't bother with a plan; I think about the writing as I'm going along.	
6	People usually understand what I've written.	
7	I see producing a written report as an important piece of work and set aside time to do it properly.	
8	I try to have a reader in mind when I write something.	
9	I usually ask a colleague to read and comment on an important document I've written.	
10	If I don't understand something, I don't include it in the piece of writing.	

How did you score?

26–30

You understand the importance of effective business writing and are doing well, but there's always room for improvement. If you work on your basic skills you could have an even greater impact.

16–26

Although you already possess some writing skills, you lack confidence and could dramatically improve your effectiveness when producing a written document. Use the checklist on page 17 to identify specific areas where you are weak, and work at improving them.

Under 16

You shy away from writing, and it is only a matter of time before you will be badly let down by your lack of skills. Start improving now by taking a critical look at some things you have written. Continue to work on your writing style, and consider enlisting the help of a friend or co-worker who could offer some constructive criticism.

2

Identify your reader
Plan your writing
Keep it short and simple
Check and check again

How good a writer are you?
Who are you writing for?
Are you getting your message across?

How effective is your writing style?

To find out just how effective your own writing style is, take a close look at a page of something you've written; and answer the questions below. As a way to improve, you could try asking yourself these questions every time you sit down to write something. Simply doing this will bring about a dramatic change for the better in your writing style.

	Question
1	Is your message immediately obvious?
2	Work out your average sentence length. Is it 15-20 words, 21-25, over 25?
3	Does your writing contain lots of exclamation marks?
4	How many times do sentences or paragraphs start with the same word?
5	Do you use capital letters for words that don't need them? For example, "Please contact the Sales Department, quoting your Purchase Order Number." (Only the word "Please" should have a capital letter in this sentence.)
6	Can you spot words or expressions that you use more than once? Look out particularly for such words as "actually," "basically," "generally," "really," and "very."
7	Are there any spelling mistakes?
8	Do you address the reader directly, in phrases such as, "Let us know what you think"?
9	Is there any technical jargon you haven't explained?
10	Is there anything that might offend the reader?
11	Have you tried to to be humorous?

Question	Answer	Points
1	Yes	5
	No	0
2	15–20	5
	21–25	3
	over 25	0
3	No	5
	Yes	0
4	1–3	5
	4–5	3
	over five	0
5	Yes	0
	No	5
6	Yes	0
	No	5
7	One or none	5
	More than one	0
8	Yes	5
	No	0
9	Yes	0
	No	5
10	Never	5
	Possibly	0
11	No	5
	Yes	0

How did you score?

Over 40
Your writing style is mostly clear and easy to follow but could be even better with a little care.

25 to 40
You're half way there but must take more time over your written communication.

Under 25
Your writing is difficult to follow, and you are hiding behind jargon and long sentences.

LEARNING FROM YOUR ANSWERS
Analyse your own writing to identify the areas for improvement.

- [ ] The message should be obvious.
- [ ] Sentences and paragraphs should be kept short.
- [ ] Opening words of sentences and paragraphs should vary.
- [ ] Repetition of words and phrases should be minimized.
- [ ] The style of language should be matched to the audience, and any techical terms explained.
- [ ] Spelling, punctuation, and grammar should be checked.
- [ ] Address the reader directly. "Let us know what you think" is better than, "Your views would be greatly appreciated."
- [ ] Don't try to be funny. Humor in writing is very difficult to carry off and can be misunderstood.
- [ ] Avoid language that might offend your reader.

Know your reader

The key to successful business writing is knowing for whom you are writing. If you can identify with your reader, you will use the right tone and the right level of information – neither too simple nor too sophisticated – and you are much more likely to get the result you want.

If it is not obvious for whom you are writing, think through the following questions to paint a clearer picture.

Are they male or female?

You should always avoid using sexist language, but if you know your audience is either entirely male or female you can afford to concentrate on that group. A catalog of maternity wear, for example, will be read mainly by women.

How old are they?

Age may be relevant to both the tone and content of your writing. For example, if you're writing material for a recruitment drive aimed at college graduates, you will be more successful if you mention people students have heard of and a lifestyle they desire. If you want to employ more mature staff, alluding to pop stars, television programs and personalities, or fashion labels they are unfamiliar with will only alienate them.

Are they part of your organization?

Co-workers will understand how your company operates; outsiders won't. A letter to a supplier, for example, might have to explain which manager is responsible for a particular part of the business or who has authority to place orders over a certain value.

What is their cultural background?

This could include nationality, education, religion, or other beliefs. If you were writing for a mainly Muslim audience, Christmas would be a poor example to give as a time of traditional family get-togethers. Likewise, an Australian audience would find it hard to identify with an image of Christmas that involves snowy weather and a roast turkey for dinner.

What is their knowledge of the subject you are writing about?

Gauging your audience's level of expertise will help you to avoid either patronizing or baffling them. If in doubt, however, it is better to explain any potentially difficult terms.

What is their income bracket?

This is important if you are hoping to sell something to your readers or if you are using examples or images that you want them to relate to. The chairman of a big company may be interested in an expensive CD player for his or her BMW; a shop assistant probably wouldn't be.

Do they have any particular interests?
Using examples from an area your readers are familiar with will help to win them over. Imagine you are the reader. For example, if you are writing a sales letter to promote a soft drink which will be mailed to subscribers to a sports magazine, you might talk about working up a thirst after a game of football; whereas, for subscribers to a gardening magazine, that thirst might occur after an afternoon spent weeding and mowing the lawn.

CONNECTING WITH YOUR READER

Remember that you are trying to build a bridge, not a barrier, with the words you write. Address your reader directly as "you" and refer to yourself as "I" or your organization as "we." Achieving the right tone takes practice. To get started, imagine that you're sitting talking to your reader across the table. Now read what you've written. Does it sound normal and conversational, or formal and stilted?
Look at the two sentences below left. The sentences on the right express the same meaning in fewer, simpler words, and in the kind of language you might use if you were chatting with someone.

THE DISTANT VOICE

"Head office prefers to send out checks to employees at the end of the calendar month."

"It is company policy to reimburse customers."

EVERYDAY LANGUAGE

"You will be paid at the end of the month."

"You will be reimbursed."

Planning and purpose

Once you have identified your audience, you need to work out why you are writing to, or for, them. If you plan the piece from the start, it will take you less time to write and will be clearer. Be clear in your mind about the message you are trying to get across to the reader.

The key message

If you're not sure exactly what message you're trying to convey, try to think of your piece of writing as an item in a newspaper. Now imagine the headline on the news story; it could be "New healthy menu for staff canteen." This is your key message.

CASE STUDY

Suppose that building work will soon start on the extension to the conference rooms at your organization's head office. The contractors suggest closing parts of the nearby parking lot in case cars are damaged by falling debris or turning equipment. To work out your key message, you need to think about what action you want to come about as a result of the communication. In this case, you want people to stop using part of the parking lot.
Key message: "Car parking switch due to building work"

Key questions:
- What: change in car parking arrangements
- Who: anyone who drives to work
- How: by moving parking spaces away from building work
- Where: rows A to C of the parking lot.
- Why: to allow building work to be carried out safely
- When: From February 3, 2001 until further notice

MEMO
To: All car drivers
From: Security Manager
RE: Parking
Date: February 1 2001

Rows A to C of the parking lot at corporate headquarters will be closed from February 3 2001 until further notice. This is to avoid the risk of damage to cars caused by the building work being carried out at the nearby conference centre.
Anyone who cannot find a parking space should use the visitors' car park.

Getting the reader on your side

Now that you know for whom you are writing and why, you should make your writing as appealing as possible.

Be active, not passive

A good way of sounding approachable is to use the active, rather than the passive, form of a verb. The passive form turns the normal sentence structure around and makes the sentence longer (see examples below).

With the active voice, it is clear who is speaking; and there is a greater sense of immediacy.

The passive voice is anonymous and gives the impression that noone is willing to take responsibility for an action. Constantly using the passive voice will stop the reader from becoming involved.

When passive is good

Occasionally, the passive voice can be useful or appropriate.

■ To avoid placing blame on the reader, which is useful when dealing with customers. For example, "The forms have not been filled in" (passive) is less accusing than "You have not filled in the forms" (active).

■ To avoid assuming the blame: "The order was not delivered on time" (passive) is preferable to "We did not deliver the order on time" (active).

■ If you don't have all the facts about who did something: For example, "The new chief executive has been appointed" (passive) avoids saying who made the appointment, which is necessary in the active form: "The board has appointed the new chief executive."

Look at the types of expressions you use when writing something at work.
■ Is the language the kind you might use when chatting with a friend?
■ Are you using jargon?
■ Have you slipped into officialese?

ACTIVE	PASSIVE
Our company won the award for best training.	The award for best training was won by our company.
Many builders will use the new material.	The new material will be used by many builders.
Proper safety measures could prevent a repeat of this kind of accident.	A repeat of this kind of accident could be prevented by using proper safety measures.

Getting the reader on your side

Being direct

When you speak, being direct comes naturally – especially when giving a command. Imagine that you're coaching a sports team: you need to convey instructions as quickly and directly as possible. In this situation you would give clear orders. You might shout something like: "Watch your back," or "Jump for the ball."

But, somehow, what comes easily when speaking becomes convoluted and difficult to understand when you try to put it on paper. There is no need to dress up what you are saying. Don't feel uncomfortable about giving orders or instructions in writing.

Using the imperative

The form of a verb that is used to give an order is called the imperative. The imperative can make your writing more punchy, especially if you use it after a long sentence. It is particularly appropriate for giving instructions; for example, "Put the check and form in the envelope provided." This is much clearer and more direct than: "The check and form should be placed in the envelope provided."

STRAIGHT TALKING
Official-sounding phrases such as, "in accordance with," "in respect of," "subsequent to" and "in reference to" simply obscure meaning and distance the reader. Many people think that packing their writing with these pompous expressions will give it greater authority. Usually the opposite is true. Consider the following example:

- What they said: "High-quality learning environments are a necessary precondition for facilitation and enhancement of the ongoing learning process."
- What they really meant: "Children need good schools if they are to learn properly."

(Source: Plain English Campaign)

Avoid being rude

There is always a possibility that giving orders in this way could sound rude, particularly if you are writing to a customer. To avoid this, simply add the word "please," as in "Please put the check and form in the envelope provided."

Making it clear: the fog index

Too many long sentences and words can make writing "foggy," or unclear. Unfortunately many people, particularly when they are writing something for business purposes, deliberately use long sentences and words to make themselves sound more authoritative. The result is more likely to be a muddled and unclear piece of work that reflects badly on the writer.

Calculating your fog index

Language experts Robert Gunning and Douglas Mueller have devised a way of gauging what they call the "fog factor" of a piece of writing:

1 Pick a piece of writing that is a hundred words long.

2 Find the average sentence length (to do this, divide the number of words by the number of sentences).

3 Count the number of words with three or more syllables. Don't count proper nouns, such as London; compound nouns, such as businesswoman; hyphenated words or verbs that have three syllables due to a suffix, such as related, agreeing, advises.

4 Add the average sentence length (from Step 2) to the number of long words (from Step 3). Multiply the total by 0.4 to find your fog index.

What the figure means

The final figure represents the number of years' education needed to understand your writing.

Most newspapers have a fog index of about seven; that is, a child who has completed primary school should be able to understand them. A fog index of 12 means the writing is harder to follow and suitable for a high-school graduate. If you reach 16, only a college graduate would easily understand the text.

Perhaps you're writing for a highly sophisticated audience, in which case, it may be fine to have an index of 16. But most of the time it's better to try to lift the fog.

Style

Keep it short

Take a look at an example of your own writing. Cross out any words that aren't vital to the meaning. You will be amazed at how much punchier the piece is with fewer words.

One of the best ways to make your writing more approachable is to avoid long sentences. To see just how effective this can be, take a look at a top quality newspaper. Sentences vary in length, but most are short and punchy. Paragraphs are only a few sentences long. You can normally tell from the first sentence or paragraph exactly what the story is about.

As another example of how you can be clear and concise without talking down to your audience, take a look at some of the best writers of books for young adults. Children are among the most demanding of audiences as they have a short attention span and won't tolerate being patronized. Successful authors captivate their audiences with concise sentences spiced up with the imaginative use of words.

Make the words work

Every word you write should be there for a reason. Using more and longer words will make your writing fuzzier, not more impressive. Look out in particular for the following bad habits.

- **Repeated words**
  Most people have a tendency to use certain favorite words all the time. Typical examples are "basically" and "literally." Can you identify any such pet words in your own writing? Are they necessary to the meaning? Is there a better alternative, or could you get rid of them altogether?

- **Stock phrases and clichés**
  We all resort to over-used phrases, such as "at the end of the day," "in a nutshell," and "level playing field." Again, look at examples of your own writing and ask yourself whether you use such phrases frequently. Do they add to the meaning? Are you using them as a succinct way to sum up a situation, or just out of laziness? Be tough on yourself when hunting for clichés.

HUMOUR

Humor should be used sparingly in business writing – if at all. Written jokes can fall flat for several reasons.
- The cues that tell someone you're joking when you're face to face – voice, facial expressions, and body language – are absent on paper. You could offend someone who thinks you're serious.
- "In" jokes usually leave some people feeling left out.
- You have to know someone well to judge their sense of humor.
- It's harder to tell a joke to a large group of people.
- Trying to be funny can detract from your central message.
- If you frequently resort to humor, people may find it difficult to take you seriously.

Using appropriate language

Jargon is language that is familiar only to a specific group of people. It makes sense to use jargon if you are sure that your audience will understand it. If wrongly used, however, jargon makes your text difficult or even impossible to understand or, at the very least, makes the reader feel left out.

Scientists, lawyers, and computer professionals are particularly prone to using jargon, but anyone who works in a specialized field should be on guard against it.

There is no reason why specialized subjects cannot be written about in a straightforward way. Newspapers, such as the *Financial Times* and the *Wall Street Journal*, for example, pride themselves on their ability to present complex information in easy-to-understand English. Both papers have many readers with a high degree of technical knowledge; yet they still take pains to explain terms that might be unfamiliar to the general reader.

Acronyms and abbreviations

Acronyms, words made up from the initial letters of other words (such as NATO for North Atlantic Treaty Organization) and abbreviations (such as GM for genetically modified), can be particularly annoying to a reader who is not familiar with them. If in doubt, spell out the acronym the first time you use it, and then go on to use the abbreviated form.

Foreign expressions should be treated as jargon and avoided unless absolutely necessary.

SPELL IT OUT OR NOT?

Take into account who your audience is likely to be when spelling out an acronym. For example, it would be very odd to spell out British Broadcasting Corporation the first time BBC was used in a television listings magazine for sale in the UK. However, it would be helpful to an American reader to be told what BBC stands for.

Sometimes spelling out the acronym is not enough; and it is necessary to give an explanation to help the reader. For example, suppose a research establishment thinks it has found a faster and cheaper way of analyzing DNA, which could be used in criminal investigations. When writing a press release about their findings, telling the reader that DNA stands for deoxyribonucleic acid would not help. It would be necessary to give a brief definition such as "a substance present in every cell in our bodies, which is unique to each individual and provides a genetic fingerprint."

Avoiding offence

You have worked hard to win over your readers by improving your writing style. Don't risk losing them through a careless choice of words.

Your organization may have a policy on the use in written material of certain words and phrases. For example, the company may prefer the use of "physically challenged" to "handicapped," or "first" or "given" rather than "Christian" name.

Trying not to offend is not simply about the words you use, however. As you write, be aware of the content of your message, as well.

Appearance

There is almost never a good reason to mention someone's appearance. One situation where people fall into this trap is when they write about women. It might seem inoffensive to refer to a female executive as a "flame-haired financial wizard," but would you expect to see a male director described in similar terms?

Personal circumstances

Details about a person, such as age, marital status, health, or activities outside work are rarely relevant. In some instances you might consider such information appropriate, for example, when introducing a new employee in the company newsletter. However, always check with the person concerned first, and make sure that your policy is consistent.

Race

A person's race rarely needs to be mentioned, unless it is impossible to say what you need to say without doing so – if you're writing about, or to, a specific racial group, for example.

Gender

Treat both sexes in the same way as far as possible. Use similar titles for both sexes. If a man is "Mr" give any female the title of "Mrs," "Miss," or "Ms." If you use a first name for one, then use it for both. Don't specify gender unless necessary. For example, do not say "male nurse" unless you would also say "female nurse."

NON-SEXIST LANGUAGE

- Don't use gender-specific terms such as "chairman." Examples of non-sexist terms include: chairperson, spokesperson, layperson, firefighter, police officer.
- Use "he or she" or "he/she" rather than constantly saying "he." Alternatively, although it is not grammatically accurate, it is easier to use "they." For example, "The team leader should be given a copy of the report so that they can make any necessary amendments."
- Use examples from both sexes. "The man who has won the lottery, the woman who has been left a legacy…"

Grammar

Poor grammar gives a bad impression and can distract or mislead. For example, consider the following advertisement: "Computer for sale by finance director with small memory." Placing the adjectival phrase, "with small memory" away from the noun it describes suggests the finance director has difficulty remembering things.

Invest in a good grammar book, and refer to it regularly to avoid making similar mistakes. For some of your readers, grammar is very important.

Common errors

Avoid the common grammatical errors that crop up in business writing, and you'll make your writing even clearer.

- **Different**
  "Different from," not "different to."

- **Who/whom**
  Use "who" when it is the subject, "whom" when it is the object, for example, "Who is at the door?" "Whom should I give this to?"

- **Less/fewer**
  Use "less" for an amount of a single item ("there's less sand in this bucket"); use "fewer" for several items ("five items or fewer").

THE RIGHT WORD

- Disinterested means impartial, not uninterested.
- Implied means suggested or indicated; inferred means deduced from evidence. "Working as a teacher implies that she likes children." "Because she works as a teacher, we inferred that she likes children."
- Unique means without equal, the only one of its kind. It is therefore incorrect to say "most unique" or "very unique."

- **That/which**
  Use "that" when the information that follows is essential to the sentence, for example, "We must start work on the order that was placed on Sunday." Use "which" when the information that follows is descriptive but not essential to the sense. The clause containing "which" is set apart by commas, for example, "The order, which was placed on Sunday, will take three months to fill."

Nouns as verbs

Turning nouns into verbs usually sounds awkward, even though the alternative is longer. Compare the following:
- "The fall in the yen impacted on the electronics industry."
- "The fall in the yen had an impact on the electronics industry."

Punctuation

Properly used, punctuation will serve to clarify your meaning. Many people get confused about punctuation, particularly the use of the apostrophe; but there are just a few simple rules to learn. You'll soon realize just how distracting bad punctuation can be.

PUNCTUATION MARK	PROPER USE	EXAMPLES
Apostrophe	a) to show that two words have been joined together b) to show possession. However, there is no apostrophe in "its" – as in, "The product has had its day." "It's" means "it is."	"You are" becomes "you're." "Ann's book"
Colon	a) to introduce a list b) before a sentence that expands on what you have just said	"Snow White's dwarves were: Sleepy, Dopey, ..." "The rain was heavy: all but three of the houses were flooded."
Commas	For short pauses within a sentence. If you can't decide whether you need one, read the passage aloud to see whether the pause is natural.	"If the market research has been done well, we can expect an excellent response to this mailing."
Semicolons	To join sentences that could function independently but are closely linked	"I wrote to inform the chairman of the results; he said he was unhappy with them."
Exclamation marks	Use only when you want to show something remarkable has happened or that you're making a joke. Use sparingly.	"There has been a terrible accident!"
Quotation marks	Commas, periods, and exclamation marks go inside quotation marks. The only exception is if the quoted word or words are placed within another sentence.	"The invoice was late," he said. "I don't expect it to happen again." "She was said to be 'furious,' but she seemed quite calm to me."

Spelling

Misspellings can make even the most painstakingly planned and well written document look unprofessional; so check spelling carefully, using a dictionary.

If you feel your spelling is poor, make a list of words you often misspell, keep it in your desk or carry it in your purse or wallet, and study it when you have a spare moment.

You may find it helpful to think of tricks to help you remember certain words, for example, "There's enough room in the word accommodation for two "c"s and two "m"s. Or, if you can't remember how to spell "adamant," think of it as "Adam Ant."

COMMON MISSPELLINGS

Absence	Fulfilled
Accommodation	Guardian
Aggravate	Irrelevant
Amendment	Liaise
Appearance	Maneuver
Beginning	Omission
Changeable	Omitted
Commitment	Permanent
Consistent	Procedure
Deficient	Relevant
Deterrent	Supersede
Dissatisfied	Transferred
Embarrass	Visible

SIMILAR WORDS: DIFFERENT MEANINGS
Watch out for the following pairs of words, which are often confused, and make sure you use the correct one.

Affect (verb)	Effect (noun)
Coarse (rough)	Course (race track, onward movement, part of a meal, etc)
Principal (main, first in importance)	Principle (rule or guideline, especially moral)
Stationery (writing materials)	Stationary (standing still)

Checking your document

If you have a short piece of writing you want to check, read the words in reverse order. This will stop your brain from reading what it expects to see and not what is actually there.

Before sending off your document you should be certain you have removed any last elements that might turn the reader off. If it's an important or long piece of writing, you will probably have read it several times, which is why you need a fresh pair of eyes to look at it.

Publishers feel it is only worthwhile for the same person to proof-read a document twice; more than that, and the brain will simply read what it expects to see. You can fool it by presenting the writing in different forms, for example, by studying a printed version rather than reading your work on a computer screen. But, after a while, it becomes counter-productive to reread something over and over again.

A friend or co-worker is more likely to spot spelling mistakes and repetitions. As someone who is slightly removed from the work, this person will also be able to tell if something doesn't make sense.

BEWARE OF SPELL CHECK

The spell check on your computer is a useful tool, but it's no substitute for a human being. If you choose the wrong word but spell it the correct way, the spell check won't spot your error. It certainly won't be able to tell if you misspell someone's name, a place, or a product. And if you accidentally repeat a word, most spell checks will not notice. Use the spell check as a first line of defence against errors, but never rely on it entirely. In the following excerpt, the mistakes a spell check would not pick up are in bold.

Dear Francis

Thank you for **you're** letter of 14 December. We were very pleased to **here that that** you like the product.

Skineaze has performed well in **trails** and we expect to launch it in **Butee** this July.

Ill makes sure you **now** how it is received and how this will **effect** future marketing.

Best wishes

Stan

Business writing checklist

Connect with your reader
- Determine your audience.
- Plan your writing; know what you have to say before you start.
- Address the reader directly, using "you" and "your."
- Use the active, rather than the passive, voice.
- If you have used humor, make sure it can't be misunderstood.
- Don't alienate or offend through sexist or racist language.

Be clear and concise
- Use everyday language, not officialese (imagine you are chatting to the reader in a restaurant.)
- Avoid jargon, abbreviations, and foreign words and phrases.
- Keep sentences and paragraphs short. Vary the way you start them.
- Don't use too many clauses and subclauses.

Don't put obstacles in the reader's way
- Take special care with spelling, and don't rely on the computer spell check to catch every mistake.
- Make sure apostrophes are in the right place.
- Use capital letters and exclamation marks only where strictly necessary.
- Read a print out of your document.
- Ask someone else to read it for clarity and spelling mistakes, and decide whether it needs one more person's approval before sending it.
- Finally, read the piece out loud so that you can hear how it sounds.

THE COMUNICATION RAMP
Think of your writing as a communication ramp between your audience and you. The four parts of that ramp are:

READERSHIP
Know who your readers are and how much they know of your subject matter.

APPROACH
Think about tone, using the active voice and avoiding jargon.

MESSAGE
Decide what you want to tell your readers.

PRESENTATION
Take care with spelling, grammar, layout and length of sentences and paragraphs.

THE FOUR Ss OF WRITING STYLE

Use
SHORT SENTENCES AND PARAGRAPHS
and
SIMPLE LANGUAGE
to deliver a
STRAIGHTFORWARD MESSAGE,
and mind your
SPELLING.

3

Put it in writing
Choose an appropriate style
Save time
Manage your messages

Are you causing confusion?
Do you suffer from e-mail overload?
Can you get through to your colleagues?

Writing for colleagues

The principles of planning, tone and style outlined in *Chapter Two* are just as relevant whether you are writing to the chief executive of your largest client company or the members of your office softball team bulletin. If you get into the habit of thinking about your writing – the language and tone you use, its structure and appearance – you will improve all of your communication skills.

Why internal communications matter

Although improving the quality of your internal communications does not affect the public face of your company, it can improve your professional image and lead to increased efficiency.

An appropriate style

This is not to say that even a hastily scribbled note stuck to a computer screen should be written in perfect English. If the note is to you, and you know exactly what it means, then you are writing effectively: you know your audience, and you've used the appropriate words.

Similarly, the tone and style of written communications within an advertising or music industry office would probably be more relaxed than in a legal or accounting department. The advertising and music businesses communicate in different ways; they thrive on creativity and originality. A bulletin board in either of these two businesses would probably carry messages in a completely different style than other industries. However, if the writer has judged the audience well, the message should get through. In both cases, a notice about fire regulations must be serious and easily understood, while a reminder of someone's leaving party can afford to be lighter in tone.

DOES YOUR ORGANIZATION COMMUNICATE WELL?

Make a list of the written messages you see when you enter your place of work. Include the reception area, hallways, noticeboards, meeting rooms, the main work place, and even the rest room.

- Do they reflect the sort of image your organization wants to convey?
- Would you be happy for a customer to see all of them?
- Do they make immediate sense?
- Are any of them offensive – whether intentionally so or not?
- Is the spelling correct?
- Is the grammar correct?

How good are your internal communications?

1 When you write notes to yourself do you often forget what you meant?

2 Do the minutes you take at a meeting sometimes lead to disagreements?

3 When you put a notice up on the noticeboard, do people often not bother to read it?

4 Do you find staff assessments difficult to write?

5 Have you ever offended anyone with a piece of internal communication?

6 Do you often have to send out the same message more than once?

7 Are the memos you send longer than those sent by your colleagues?

8 Do you send "urgent" messages on the internal e-mail system (intranet) at least once a day?

9 When deciding who should see a particular message, do you tend to think "If in doubt, send it"?

10 When you use e-mail, do you usually send your message to large groups of people, or even to the whole organization?

ASSESSING YOUR ANSWERS

If you answered "yes" to more than four questions, you are not giving enough thought to how you communicate with your co-workers. You need to decide who your readers are, what you want to tell them, and how urgent the message is.

Taking more care with the words you use and planning your written communications in advance should help to make your writing clearer.

At the moment you are too quick to dash off a memo or e-mail without thinking through the consequences. This doesn't save you time in the long run because you often have to clarify your original message. You are making life difficult for others, too, by bombarding them with messages and information that may not be relevant to them.

Recording meetings

Meetings play an important part in most managers' working lives, but they are only really effective if everyone agrees on what was discussed and agreed upon. The minutes of the meeting are a written record of what was said and provide a way of measuring progress against clearly defined goals.

Many meetings become quite heated. If you are taking the minutes, you must make sure that you record what is said in a fair and balanced way. You may want to contribute to the discussion yourself; but, if you do, make sure that you do not lose track of what is being said.

Format

There are several ways of presenting minutes, and your organization may have its own procedures. Certain elements should always be included, however.

- Names of those present
- Apologies from anyone who couldn't attend.
- Where and when the meeting took place
- Anything discussed that was not on the agenda
- Main issues discussed and any decisions made
- Details of what action is to be taken and by whom
- Date of next meeting (if appropriate)

Avoid misunderstandings

It is important that the minutes that come from a meeting are accurate and easy to understand, or they may cause disagreement or misunderstanding.

- Jot down notes as you go along, and write up the minutes as soon after the meeting as possible.
- Write in the simple past tense – "Mrs. Flynn said that ..."
- If you're unclear about what has been said or decided, ask the chairperson if you can summarize the point before the meeting moves on.

SAMPLE AGENDA
A formal meeting follows a written agenda which also provides the format for the minutes.

Agenda for meeting of the County Arts Department – Literature Working Group on 2 March 2000.

1. Apologies.
2. Minutes of last meeting.
3. Matters arising.
4. Progress and evaluation of workshops.
5. Poetry competition.
7. Any other business.
8. Date of next meeting.

- Ask for names and places to be spelled out and dates, times, and amounts confirmed.
- If an area of discussion seems particularly sensitive or confidential, ask how the group would like it recorded, if at all. Make sure you know what to leave out, as well as what to include.
- Be tactful; people can be very touchy about how you record their comments or describe their projects. The chairperson usually reads the minutes before you circulate them and can spot anything that might upset someone.

Taking notes

Don't try to write the minutes during the meeting. Your priority should be to take down the main points and leave putting them into the right style until afterwards.

To keep your notes clear, you may find it helpful to number the points that are discussed as you go along. You could also add notes to yourself in square brackets. For example, "[sensitive]" could remind you to be careful how you word a particular point. With practice, you will probably develop your own form of "shorthand," for example, "OR" for "off the record" (not to be recorded) or "S" for "sensitive".

SAMPLE MINUTES

Minutes of the meeting of County Arts Department: Literature Working Group held at Cromwell House, March 2 2000 at 3.00p.m.

Present: John Beerman, Viv Goodwin (secretary), Alice Thomson, Tom Winter (chairman).

1. Apologies
Jenny Hill

2. Minutes of the last meeting
These were agreed upon

3. Old business
All on the agenda

4. Progress and evaluation of workshops
It was agreed to postpone evaluation until the end of the series

5. Poetry competition
John Beerman said Bunty's Bakery is eager to sponsor the event again; he will pursue this. The competition will be in October (deadline for entries is August 1). The budget was discussed.
ACTION: JB

5. New business
Tom Winter said the county was offering arts and disability training and asked which days would be most convenient for the Literature Working Group. Saturday morning was agreed upon as the best time.
ACTION: TW

5. Date of next meeting
April 2 2000 at 3.00p.m. hours at Cromwell House.

Appraisals and disciplinary procedures

KEEPING UP TO DATE
In an annual appraisal, there is a danger of focusing only on the recent past. To avoid this, it is helpful to write brief interim reports noting any circumstances or events that may have affected your staff's performance – perhaps every three or six months.

Even the most skilled communicators can become tongue-tied when it comes to commending or criticizing their peers. It can be difficult to comment on the performance of someone you work with.

Appraisals

Because assessments by their very nature may include criticism, and are often linked to salary increases and promotion, they must be handled with great care and sensitivity.

As with minutes, it is important that all parties concerned feel the written record accurately reflects the discussion that took place. Both manager and employee should sign the written appraisal to confirm that they consider it accurate.

DISCIPLINARY PROCEDURE

- Follow your organization's standard procedures when taking disciplinary action against someone.
- Tell your line manager what you are doing and take his or her advice. Also consult the Human Resources Department.
- Keep written notes of incidents that necessitate any form of disciplinary action and subsequent exchanges between those involved. These will be vital in case of a grievance or litigation.

As well as writing up the appraisal, keep a note of any points in which you have agreed to follow up.

Do not use the appraisal form to record disciplinary warnings. These should be dealt with separately.

Giving a written warning

A written warning should be clear and to the point. It should stick to the facts and omit any opinion or subjective judgment. Be straightforward and unemotional. Avoid trying to "soften the blow" with a lighthearted remark. This will send out confusing signals, and the person involved may then underestimate the seriousness of the situation.

- State the problem.
- Give examples of how this has affected the employee's work.
- Mention any previous warnings.
- State what improvements you wish to see, giving specific targets and deadlines if possible.
- State the consequences if the improvements are not made and maintained.

Remember that this is a confidential document, but it is still wise to ask your boss and someone in the Human Resources Department to review what you have written.

Writing memos

Memos are short and concise communications, usually for internal circulation only, which may be sent to one or more recipients.

Although e-mails have replaced memos in many organizations, they remain a valuable way of communicating. A piece of paper is harder to ignore than an e-mail and is usually seen as being more important. Memos should not, however, be used as a way to avoid talking to someone.

Format

Try to keep memos short; stick to one page. The following headings should appear, double spaced, at the top of the memo. They provide a lot of information in a short space and allow the memo itself to be more concise.

TO:

FROM:

DATE:

SUBJECT:

Composing the message

The best memos deal with just one topic. If you're covering more ground, number each point.

Decide on your message by framing a headline that sums it up. Now, answer the key questions in your piece of writing: what, who, why, how, where and when. Think about what action you want to come about as a result of the communication. If you are informing people that something is going to happen or asking for a task to be done, always give a deadline. Try to end on a positive note.

Sending copies

If you decide to send the memo to people other than those directly affected by it, add "cc:" (originally an abbreviation for carbon copy) or "c:" at the bottom, followed by the names or titles of the people concerned.

You may want to copy a memo to someone without letting the recipient know that you have done so – perhaps if you are carrying out a particularly sensitive correspondence and would like your manager to be informed of it. In this case, add "bc:" at the bottom of the copy only, followed by the name of the person whom you are copying.

Send copies only to those who really need or want to see this memo. Some people like to be informed of what's going on; others will be too busy to read the memo. Use your own judgment to decide who needs a copy.

Memos are particularly effective for:
- marking a shift in policy
- summing up a meeting
- reminding people of something
- imposing a deadline
- squelching a rumor

Writing memos

Case study

Suppose your company has decided that each department should apply for an internationally recognized certificate of quality or accreditation and you have to compose a memo to inform staff.

- Headline: Team to boost sales through new working methods
- What? Raising standards
- Who? Team leaders
- Why? To win international accreditation and boost sales
- How? By improving working practices and skills
- Where? Within the automotive components department and, ultimately, the whole organization
- When? Over an 18-month period (In this case you want the team leaders to begin a process that will lead to international accreditation.)
- Action: All team leaders to draw up plans of how they will achieve accreditation and attend meeting on the date and at the time specified

---

MEMO

TO: Team leaders in Automotive Components Division
FROM: Divisional Director
RE: International accreditation
DATE: February 3 2001

Autoboost has decided that each department will apply for international accreditation as part of its drive to improve sales. Accreditation will raise standards and increase the company's skills base. It may also mean changes to working practices.

The human resources department will send out details of how to apply for accreditation. Team leaders will be responsible for drawing up a plan for how their team can achieve this.

A meeting will be held at 11 a.m. on February 10 for team leaders to discuss the strategy. The board believes accreditation will improve working standards and help us to boost sales both at home and abroad.

cc: Board of directors

Using e-mail

Because e-mails are frequently dashed off at high speed, often little thought is given to their construction. But e-mails reflect both you and your organization just as much as a letter on your personal note paper.

The best way to think of a business e-mail is as another form of memo. In fact, in many offices the e-mail has completely replaced the memo. Yet, many companies still don't have a policy on e-mail style and use, leaving their organizations commercially and even legally vulnerable, as well as threatening their productivity.

Big brother is watching you

Despite the illusion of intimacy, e-mail is not a private way of communicating. You may think you've deleted a message, but a computer expert will be able to retrieve it.

If you're using your employer's equipment, they have the right to "eavesdrop" on your e-mail, just as they can listen in on your phone calls. So, if you wouldn't be happy to see a message pinned on the bulletin board, don't put it in an e-mail. Many organizations now have their own internal e-mail system. The same cautions about privacy apply.

A handful of employees set up a special user group specifically to exchange gossip about their boss, whom they thought was unable to access the site. The boss proved them wrong on the day he left the company by sending a message out on the user group network, inviting them all to a farewell party.

SO YOU THINK E-MAILS ARE PRIVATE?

- In the UK, the Conservative Party's head of marketing and membership lost his job after a leaked speech by the deputy party leader was found in his e-mail outbox.

- An employee at a TV production company was fired after a memo about a presenter's alleged difficulty with big words appeared on a celebrity gossip website. The source of the "leak" was identified after the company checked through all of its employees' old e-mails and found that one person had been in regular contact with the website.

- Four-year-old e-mails sent by staff at Microsoft were presented as evidence against the company in its antitrust case.

- E-mails between Monica Lewinsky and Linda Tripp, detailing the intern's affair with President Clinton, were used in the Supreme Court hearing.

- In the USA, e-mails are regularly used in divorce and custody hearings.

Using e-mail

Style

E-mails are written in a wide range of styles. Some people write in a way that is so casual it is almost a form of shorthand: "How r u? Speak soon, Blacksox." Others adopt a letter format, but don't take the same care over spelling and grammar that they would when writing on paper.

E-mails should be short and punchy, like memos. Remember the four Ss when writing an e-mail: keep it Short, Simple, and Straightforward, and Spell correctly. E-mails are normally read quickly and need to be easily understood.

However, make sure your message doesn't sound abrupt. If you are using an internal message system on which just the first line of a message will appear at the top of someone's screen, consider how it will be understood.

The subject line

This is the blank area below the name and address of the person to whom you are sending the e-mail. It serves the same purpose as the subject line in a memo. Use a precise subject that tells readers exactly what the e-mail is about. If you are vague, they may not bother to read it. There is a limit to the number of characters you can use in the subject line of some e-mail systems.

A vague subject such as "recent meeting" won't grab the attention of someone who attends countless meetings. "Breakthrough in grant appeal" is much more eye-catching.

If you send several e-mails in a correspondence about one topic, use the same subject line for each so that they are easier to file. Don't put "urgent" unless it really is or people soon won't take you seriously.

Threads

This is a way of linking several, connected e-mails. When the person replies to your e-mail by clicking on the "reply" icon rather than creating a new message, the original subject line is retained, making it easier to follow the thread of the discussion.

The thread will break down when it is used for too long, or when the discussion has moved on.

Signature

This is the "letterhead" of your e-mail: a few lines that appear at the bottom of every message. A signature should include: your name, title, e-mail address, company name, phone and fax numbers and website address. You can set your signature up and save it so that it can be inserted with a single click or keystroke.

Good practice

- Like memos, e-mails should be filed, along with any replies, either as print-outs or stored on disk.
- If you receive a message that you feel is offensive, tell your manager immediately. The sender may not realize the effect their message has had and should be told.
- Most internal e-mail systems allow you to send your message to everyone in the organization at once; use this facility sparingly. Think who really needs the information. You'll save everyone else time and prevent important messages from getting lost among trivia.
- Don't use emoticons – symbols to convey the writer's mood – such as :-) for a smile. Many people find them childish and irritating; others have no idea what they mean. Receiving an e-mail peppered with symbols you don't understand can be annoying and can transform a serious e-mail into something quite frivolous.

E-MAIL AND THE LAW
Since e-mail is still relatively new, the law surrounding it is hazy. It's safest to treat an e-mail, even one sent on an internal system, like any other form of published material.

The British insurance company, Norwich Union was one of the first organizations to learn this when it was forced to pay out $700,000 in damages to its rival, Western Provident Association, over allegations that circulated in its internal e-mail system.

- E-mail has its own vocabulary of acronyms, such as BTW (by the way) and FWIW (for what it's worth). As with all acronyms, avoid using these unless you are sure that your reader will understand them.
- Spell correctly.
- Don't type words all in capital letters as this is the e-mail equivalent of shouting.

DON'T:
- send derogatory e-mails
- conduct an office romance by e-mail
- put confidential or commercially sensitive information in an e-mail
- be racist or sexist (while you may think your message is light-hearted, others may not agree.)
- spread unlawful or defamatory material

Avoiding e-mail overload

**DOES E-MAIL RULE
YOUR BUSINESS LIFE?**

■ Do you check your
e-mails more
than once every
two hours?

■ Do you receive more
than five personal
e-mails a day?

■ Do you prefer to
handle difficult
situations by
e-mail?

■ Do you use e-mails
as your main way
of staying in touch
with friends?

■ Do you find it
difficult
to end an
e-mail
conversation?

If you answered "yes"
to more than one of the
above questions, e-mail
plays too big a part in
your business life.

Used well, e-mail can boost productivity and save time. However, the ease of e-mail means that it can be overused, with a disproportionate amount of time spent composing, sending, checking for, and reading messages.

How to keep e-mail under control

Set aside certain times of the day to check your e-mail; three times is usually adequate.

Consider disabling the function on your computer that tells you as soon as you have mail, so that you don't drop everything to read it.

A bit of e-mail banter with a customer or colleague can be an important way of building a relationship; but make sure it isn't taking up too much time.

Many offices treat personal e-mails like non-work phone calls: they're allowed, but within reason. If you don't have a policy to follow, use your common sense.

Don't overload systems by sending too many attachments.

Ask yourself how you would have communicated a message before e-mail existed. If the answer is that you wouldn't have bothered, then don't send the e-mail.

If someone doesn't reply to an e-mail immediately, don't resend the message. They may check their mail at set times, and will feel as if you are hounding them if you keep sending the same message.

If your message is urgent, follow it up with a phone call, or consider phoning rather than e-mailing.

WHAT DO USERS THINK OF E-MAIL?
In a survey of 150 businesses in the London area:

■ Nearly 80 percent of people said they read e-mail as soon as it arrives.
■ Fifteen percent of companies said their systems crashed once a week due to e-mail overload.
■ Over half said an e-mail had caused them offence or confusion.
■ More than 80 percent thought e-mail was used when verbal communication would have been more effective.

(Source: London-based computer training company In Tuition.)

Internal publications

Writing an article for an internal publication is an effective way of raising your own profile, especially since many of the bigger in-house magazines have a readership far beyond the organization's workforce. Don't wait to be asked. Most editors are desperate for contributions and will be delighted to hear any suggestions.

Readership

Check with the editor to find out who receives the magazine. The readership might include former employees, retirees, major clients, suppliers, or potential clients. Bear in mind as you write that not every reader will be up to date with how the organization is run, and you may have to spell out changes.

Timing

Most magazines are planned well in advance, so be sure that everything you're writing about will still be relevant when your article appears.

Co-ordinate

- Find out what else will appear in that issue so that you don't overlap with another article, either in content or illustrations.
- Suggest cross-references to related articles in the same issue.

- Review what has appeared about your subject in earlier issues of the magazine in order to prevent duplication of information.
- Discuss with the editor whether you could justify a series of articles on different aspects of a single topic.

Purpose

Before you start writing, be clear in your mind what your article aims to achieve. Common reasons for writing an article are: to highlight new issues in the industry; to inform colleagues of a change (in policy, law, work practise, or product range, for example); to ask for others opinion; to boost morale (for example, with news of a charity success, award, or celebrity visit); and to entertain.

Common reasons for writing an article

- To tell employees about a change (in policy, law, or working practise, for example).
- To ask their opinion.
- To boost morale (with news of a charity success, award, or celebrity visit).
- To entertain.

FINDING A NEW SPIN

You can add interest to your feature article by presenting it in a different way. For example:
- diary of a deal or product development
- case study
- day in the life of someone to show the importance of that person's role within the organization
- the team behind a product, project, or successful deal

4

Seeking information
Persuading the reader
Letters that get a response
Getting letters published

Are your letters effective?
When is a letter appropriate?
How can a letter get results?

How to write a letter

A good letter can boost business, help prevent a crisis and improve your personal standing. A poor letter can waste time, cause confusion, and damage your relationship with a supplier or customer.

Letter format

If you are not using a corporate letterhead, put your address at the top right hand corner. Immediately beneath this add any further contact details, such as your telephone number and extension, cellular phone number, fax number, and e-mail address.

The name and title of the person you are writing to should be on the left-hand side, starting a few lines below the end of your address, and followed by their address.

Keep punctuation to a minimum unless your organization's policy states otherwise.

- Write the date in the format October 5 2000, and put it either two lines below your address or two lines above the recipient's address.
- Don't indent either address or put commas after each line.
- Use a colon after "Dear" at the beginning of the letter and a comma after "Sincerely" at the end.
- Use periods after abbreviations.
- You may want to include a subject line at the top of the main text, for example, "Re: Frankfurt Trade Fair."

When you send a fax

- Always use a cover sheet, which should include your name, phone number and address, the date and the number of pages you are faxing.
- State who to contact if the fax is not transmitted properly.

If the document is confidential, consider other ways of sending it – perhaps by courier or e-mail (although the latter is not entirely safe) –or telephone the recipient and alert him or her that a fax is on its way.

CHECKLIST FOR LETTER WRITING

- Do you know to whom you are writing – even if you don't have a name?
- Have you planned the points you want to make, or answer?
- Does your letter establish a rapport with the reader?
- Have you used simple language?
- Are there any unnecessary repetitions?
- Do your points follow a logical order?
- Have you supported your points with evidence or examples?
- Does your letter end on an upbeat note?
- Does anyone else need to see the letter before you send it?
- Can you summarize the main purpose of your letter in one sentence?

Are you a successful letter writer?

A well-written letter is an efficient business tool and should produce results. If your letters typically go unanswered or the recipients have to phone you to ask what you meant, don't do what you ask, get it wrong, or fail to do it by the required date, the problem could be with your letter-writing.

Look back over some of the letters you have written and which have failed to produce the response you were hoping for. Perhaps you have slipped into a style that doesn't encourage the recipient to reply or leaves them confused about the purpose of the letter. If you had received the letter, how would you have responded?

LETTER-WRITING PROBLEMS AND SOLUTIONS

PROBLEM	POSSIBLE REASON	SOLUTION
No reply	You sent it to the wrong person, or the person you wrote to has changed jobs.	Call in advance to make sure you're sending the letter to the right person; check the spelling of his or her name, title, and whether that person will be in the office when you expect the letter to arrive.
	You didn't encourage the person to reply.	Make it worthwhile to reply. Use incentives: if you're asking them for information for a survey, for example, you could offer to send a copy of the results.
	You didn't make it easy to reply.	Ensure it's as easy as possible to reply. If you don't know the person, this may mean sending a stamped addressed envelope, reply card or an 800 number.
An inadequate reply	You didn't make it clear what you were asking; perhaps you weren't direct enough.	Make sure you are clear in your own mind about what you want the letter to achieve. Don't be afraid to ask direct questions. If you are raising several points give each one a numbered paragraph.
They didn't reply in time.	You didn't give the recipient a deadline.	Always state a deadline by which you expect a specified action or a reply. Present easy-to-understand reasons for doing something by a certain date.
	The deadline was unrealistic.	If the deadline is too far off, the person may be tempted to put your letter to one side, where it will probably become buried under a pile of other requests. If the deadline is too close, he or she may feel you are being unreasonable.

Requesting information

By providing the right amount of information, you make it easier for your request to be answered. If you offer too much information, the person may simply delay answering your letter. Too little information may result in a standard reply.

A request for information may seem like one of the easiest types of letters to write; but if you are not certain about what you need, the request may quickly turn into a paperchase of further requests and counter-requests.

Ask directly for what you want
Be specific about dates, quantities, product numbers, and so on.

Explain why you need it
This will help the person dealing with your request make sure that you receive exactly what you want.

If you've asked for a price quote for a piece of machinery, explain how you intend to use the equipment.

When people know exactly why you want something, they may be able to supply useful extra information. For example, if you ask for a quote for a particular piece of waterproof material and explain that it is for a new line of yachting clothing your company is working on, the supplier might suggest that you try a newly available material, which is designed specifically to withstand sea water.

The reasons you want the information may affect the other person's willingness to supply it. For example, if you are requesting some commercially sensitive information, specifying that it is for private research may make it more likely that your request will be met.

Be clear about timelines
State whether there is any deadline.

Spell out any benefits to the reader
Let the reader know if meeting your request will produce any tangible benefits. For example, you may be considering placing a large order subject to a satisfactory price, or providing them with a credit or some publicity in return for their help.

End with a thank-you
Courtesy makes it more likely that the reader will take the trouble to meet your requests and will make it easier to follow up with a later inquiry.

Delivering a straightforward message

This is not a "hard sell" sort of letter, but you still want the reader to pay attention to the information it contains.

Get the reader's attention

When you send a letter, you are competing with all the "junk mail" that arrives on your reader's desk, as well as all the other demands on their time.

Your letter has only about 20 seconds in which to grab the reader's attention, so a strong opening paragraph is vital. Try to get to the point and capture attention right away, perhaps by telling them something new or exciting.

Deliver your message

Make your most important point as soon as possible, and do not hide your message among unnecessary information.

Counter any negatives

Try to anticipate any possible questions or negative aspects your message might carry for the reader. If there are solutions or counterarguments, present them. Dispelling readers' fears will make them more receptive to your message.

THIS WELL WRITTEN LETTER WAS SENT BY THE MANAGING DIRECTOR OF A SWIMWEAR COMPANY TO A FACTORY MANAGER

Dear Belinda:

Market research has shown us that June is now our peak selling period: sales are ten percent higher in this month than any other. **[Attention grabber]**

To avoid running out of stock this year, the board of directors has decided to introduce Sunday shifts during the month leading up to this peak period. Of course, not everyone will want to work Sundays **[Possible negative]**, but we will be offering a flexible compensation package made up of generous over-time payments and extra days off. **[Counter negative]**

I will be sending you details about this package closer to its implementation, but I wanted you to know that we have been giving a great deal of thought to how we could make the workload more even in the period preceding this busy time of year. **[Win over the reader]**

Sunday shifts will make sure we can meet orders and therefore boost sales, which is good news for everyone, especially now that we have introduced profit sharing. **[Upbeat ending]**

Best wishes

Tim Hardy

The persuasive letter

Persuasion is an art; and, in a letter, success depends on following the rules of good business writing: get to the point, use the active voice, make your sentences short and punchy, and keep your paragraphs brief. In addition, try to do the following:

- Establish rapport.
- Appeal to the reader directly by explaining why it is in his or her interests to continue reading.
- Explain how you are both working towards the same goal or have a common problem that you can help solve.
- Reassure the reader of your good will.

The letter on the opposite page is both persuasive and well written. The writer has taken care to plan the letter, to vary the length and structure of his sentences, and to counter any worries his reader might have. He opens the letter with a fact that is bound to grab the reader's attention. He then mentions a common concern in order to build rapport between writer and reader.

Next, he suggests a solution to the shared problem. He reassures the reader and then tells him what action he would like him to take, giving him an incentive for doing so. The letter ends with two upbeat statements.

THE POSTSCRIPT
The postscript, or PS, is a useful tool. It allows you to alter the tone of your letter without the change seeming too abrupt.

If you've written a serious letter, which may leave the writer feeling a little uneasy, a postscript can lighten the mood and help you end on an upbeat note. A postscript is also another way of keeping your reader's attention.

However, don't use a postscript to convey a key piece of information. If the information is important, it should be in the main body of the letter – not tagged onto the end.

Adding a handwritten PS can turn a standard letter into something more intimate. If you're sending out 20 invitations to a product launch, you could add something like, "Hope you can make it" to letters sent to people you know well.

A postscript can help to separate work and non-work subjects. It can, for example, be used to inquire about someone's family.

But don't feel you have to add a PS; do so only if it seems natural.

Dear Sam

Did you know that a news item related to a case of suspected food poisoning now appears in the national media, on average, once every two days? **[Attention grabber]**

We both know that any hint of a food scare can be disastrous to both the manufacturer and its suppliers. **[Mutual goal and common concern]** This is why we've decided to introduce a new food safety audit at each of our suppliers.

The audit will build on the regular checks we already make. But it will also look at ways in which we can reassure our customers that we are putting their safety first. This might, for example, mean changing the information we print on food labels. **[Suggested solution to problem]**.

As we value your years of experience in the food business and know that you already adhere to the highest standards of hygiene, we'd like to hear your views on the subject. **[Reassurance]** I will be sending you details of the proposed changes within a few days. **[Action]** Please take a look at the suggestions, and let us know what you think.

We plan to use the audit as part of a publicity campaign to reassure our customers. We thought you might make a good case study to feature in the publicity. **[Incentive]**

I look forward to discussing the proposals with you. **[Positive statement]**.

With best wishes

Gerald Balmford
Marketing Director, Dairy Delights Inc.

PS: Congratulations on your commendation in the Best Desserts Awards. I look forward to tasting the winning entry. **[End on a positive note]**

Making a complaint

Venting your anger at someone who has let you down can feel very satisfying, but the feelings of satisfaction soon fade if your outburst fails to solve your problem. You will resolve the situation faster if you take a systematic approach to your complaint.

It may be quicker and easier to resolve the issue by talking to the responsible person, either face-to-face or on the phone. However, in some instances, a letter may help clarify your thoughts and help you calm down.

Get it right

■ Investigate the complaint fully and keep a record of your findings.

■ Work out in advance how you want the problem resolved. Give the person you're complaining to a chance to correct the situation. There may be a time in the future when you need this person's cooperartion. Be specific; give deadlines and exact terms.

■ Make sure you are dealing with the right person.

■ Keep your tone straightforward. Don't be sarcastic or emotional. Stick to the facts.

■ Keep records of dates, times, who you dealt with, and what was said.

■ Keep up the pressure, and follow through any threats you make.

Effective complaining

1 Investigate, and get the facts.

2 Find out who you should be dealing with.

3 TELEPHONE: Set deadline for action.   3 WRITE: Set deadline for action.

3a Write to confirm what was agreed upon.

Satisfied   Unsatisfied   Satisfied   Unsatisfied

4 Say you will take the matter further by writing to a manager/company director, and do so.

Satisfied   Unsatisfied

5 Write saying that you will contact the union, arbitration board, trade association.

6 Only threaten legal action if you are prepared to take it.

Satisfied   Unsatisfied

7 Follow through on any threats.

Presto Printers
5100 Hampton Avenue, St. Louis, MO 63109

June 27 2000

Jim Goodman
Professional Papers Inc
5117 Industrial Way
St. Louis, MO 63132

Dear Jim:

We have been buying paper from your company for nearly two years and up till now have been very happy with the service.

Unfortunately, a delivery due on June 6 was a day late, and the paper was the wrong size. Although I phoned Jane Gooding to ask for the paper to be replaced immediately, this did not happen until June 10.

This caused us considerable disruption and expense in overtime payments. I would, therefore, like to discuss with you a reduction in payment to cover these costs. I would also like your assurance that this will not happen again.

I am sure that we can return to our previous, successful working relationship once we have resolved this matter, and I look forward to hearing from you later this week.

Sincerely yours,

Alice Jamison

Answering complaints

Everyone hates receiving a letter of complaint; but, when someone has gone to the trouble of sending a letter, that person feels strongly about the issue. A prompt and well-thought-out reply may defuse the situation.

1 Analyze the grievance

What exactly is the complaint about? Make a list of the points the writer has raised, so that you answer each of them.

2 Investigate

Talk to the relevant people within your organization so that you have their side of the story. You may decide that the matter needs to be taken higher. Perhaps the letter highlights a flaw in one of your products or the way your organization operates.

3 Write your reply

If your organization is at fault, apologize early in the letter. If the complaint is unfounded, say so firmly but politely. Your customer may simply want reassurance that their complaint has been dealt with. In other cases, some form of compensation may be in order. But before making any offer of compensation, always be sure you have authority to do so.

MAKE THE MOST OF COMPLAINTS

According to one estimate, the average person who has a complaint will tell between nine and ten people about it. This represents damaging, if free, publicity. But if you handle a complaint skilfully, your customer may well sing your praises.

An airline customer, for example, complained that his favorite golfing magazine was not available in the VIP Lounge. The airline apologized and sent him a free annual subscription to the magazine. Every time it landed on his front porch he was reminded of the airline.

A complaint is also a valuable source of customer feedback. Take the example of the North American retailer, Nordstrom, who received several complaints about the high level of artificial lighting in its Californian stores. Eventually, Nordstrom built bright and airy stores with plenty of natural light. Customers were happy, and Nordstrom also cut its fuel bills.

(Source: *Fabled Service*, by Betsy Sanders, published by Pfeiffer & Company, California, 1995.)

Letters in print

Writing to the letters page of a newspaper or magazine or to the "listeners' letters" spot on a radio show, is a good way of publicizing your organization or of expressing your point of view, if you disagree with an article.

Study the publication for an idea of the sort of letters they run, the typical length, and the topics that are normally written about. Shorter letters stand a greater chance of getting in; longer ones may be cut back ruthlessly.

Improve your chances of publication

- Supply a full return address and day-time telephone number. Many publications won't accept letters with only an e-mail address, in case you are claiming to be someone you're not.
- Specifically refer to the article you are responding to: the day it appeared, the headline, and perhaps the page number and journalist's name. This does not apply if you are writing about a topical issue.
- Include your name and title or position and any other details that give your letter extra relevance, such as a position in a local trade organization or large company.
- Respond quickly, especially if you're writing about a news story.

- E-mail will save you time. Include your address and telephone number.
- Remember that you can write to say that you agree with a letter or article.

EXAMPLE
A journalist has interviewed you for a feature on sports sponsorship. You feel you were misquoted. Here's your reply:

Dear Sir:

Although "Running ahead of the pack," May 7, gave an interesting insight into the competitive world of brand sponsorship, I feel your reporter did not represent my views accurately.

Jumping Jack Shoes, the sports footwear company of which I am marketing manager, has sponsored five major sports events locally – not a "single, token effort," as your article claimed.

We also prefer to sponsor local teams and are certainly not "disillusioned" with the Phoenix Suns. How could we be, given their present, unstoppable, form?

Yours faithfully
Martin Filler
Marketing Manager, Jumping Jack Shoes

DO'S AND DON'TS
- Don't use the letter-to-the-editor page if you have a serious complaint; rather, contact the editor directly.
- Don't rant. Newspapers like this sort of letter because it shows raw emotions. But if you're writing as the voice of an organization, an angry, emotional letter does not reflect well on your employer.
- Do make your letter measured and logical; be human, but don't forget to include facts to back up your case.
- Do end on a positive note.

Rejection letters

When you're writing a rejection letter, remember how it felt to be on the receiving end of one.

■ **Did you ever learn anything from the experience?**

■ **How did you feel about the company?**

■ **Did it make you reassess your career options?**

Writing a letter to tell someone you don't want them is hard, especially if you've gotten to know them quite well during a lengthy selection process.

It's only polite and humane to write as positive a letter as possible. It's also in your own interests to leave this candidate feeling well disposed towards you. The person you've just rejected may one day be your boss or a customer. Your first-choice candidate might change his or her mind, or you might realize that the person you rejected would be perfect for another position.

Even if none of this happens, you still want this person to go away with a positive view of you and your company.

Soften the blow

Applying for a job is a time-consuming and emotional process. Receiving a standard rejection letter with no explanation of why they weren't suitable will leave the candidate feeling angry and rejected.

Once you've made up your mind, try to let all the candidates know at the same time. This makes it less likely that they will hear from someone else and will put them out of their suspense.

What to include in the letter

■ Thank the candidate for coming in for an interview and say how much you enjoyed meeting her.

■ Let her down gently by telling her that you have decided to offer the job to someone else. If you can, explain why: the successful candidate had more experience or skills or specialist knowledge that meshed better with the team. You might even suggest that she phone you to discuss her performance further.

■ Offer a positive statement. Tell the candidate that she was on a short list of five, or that 300 people applied for the job. Praise her enthusiasm, knowledge, or bright ideas.

■ End on an upbeat note. Say that you will keep her resume on file, wish her well in her career, and thank her for her interest in your organization.

REJECTING BILL GATES

Great care should be taken when writing a rejection letter. Today's reject may be tomorrow's chief executive. Some high-flying business men and women use rejection letters to spur them on to greater things. Sometimes, they even end up in the boardroom. No one will blame you for rejecting a budding Bill Gates – as long as you do so in a polite and thoughtful way.

The personal note

Handwritten letters are the personal side of business writing. If they are used thoughtfully, they can have a huge and lasting impact on their recipients.

Personal letters are also a great way of networking and making sure that people remember you. They take longer to produce than word-processed documents because you may have to rewrite your letter several times. For this reason, they need greater planning. For a longer letter, you may find it useful to produce a draft on a word processor before writing out the final version in longhand.

When to put pen to paper

Handwritten notes or letters should be reserved for personal occasions or for when you want to acknowledge a certain type of relationship.

- To mark an employee's achievement – either in business or private life – such as winning an award, meeting a tough sales target, running a marathon, or having a baby. Imagine how touched you would be to receive a personal letter from your boss, even if you'd never met him.
- To acknowledge a tragic or difficult event, such as the death of a family member, friend, or colleague or the diagnosis of a serious illness. Writing a letter serves two purposes. It lets the reader know that you are aware of what has happened, and it shows your support and concern.
- As a thank-you. This could range from acknowledging that someone has worked particularly hard for you, or simply thanking them for taking you out to dinner or lunch. If the letter is aimed at someone within your organization, however, it may be more sensible to thank them in a more formal way so that there is a record of their achievement.
- As a way of staying in touch. Perhaps someone has been promoted, is leaving their organization or has been transferred abroad. Write to congratulate them and to say that you hope you won't lose touch. You never know when you will meet again.
- To let people know you're moving on. Use the letter to tell people where you're going and what your new job will be and to thank them for their help and friendship in the past. Even if they've already heard your news, they will appreciate a personal note from you. You could just add a handwritten message to printed change-of-address cards.

THE PERSONAL TOUCH
A handwritten note will be even more memorable if you use a fountain pen and good quality paper, although your normal, headed notepaper is equally suitable. Addressing the envelope by hand will also make it stand out from the crowd.

5

Tackling a report
Passing on information
Carrying out research
Presenting your results

What is the objective of your report?
How should you plan it?
How will you present it?

What are reports for?

Can you think of a report that particularly impressed you? What did you like about it? Was it the layout, the style of writing, the depth of research, or the convincing summary?

Writing a report can seem like a daunting proposition. The very word "report" may bring back memories of school and written assignments that you did with great reluctance. If you've been asked to write a report by someone very senior in your organization, the prospect may be even more intimidating.

But this could be your big break. It's your chance to show that you're a clear thinker and that you have ideas of your own. Many people only get noticed by their senior managers, and promoted, after they've written a report.

A report is really only a longer version of a memo. There are several reasons why you might be asked to write a report:

- To tell colleagues what took place at a conference, meeting, or visit
- To provide an update on a project or department
- To evaluate a market or other commercial opportunity

Sometimes, you won't need to do a great deal of extra research. You'll be able to write the report simply by collating information that's already at your fingertips. If the information is familiar, you must still make sure you are fulfilling the assignment given to you. And you will probably have to try harder to present it in an interesting way.

The debriefing report

This is a short report in which you pass on anything important that you have learned from a trip, visit or conference.

You don't need to include everything that happened. As always, concentrate on what will be of use to your reader. This sort of report can provide leads for your sales force about new trends, indicate potential new clients, or offer customer feedback. A debriefing report should include the following information.

- **When and where?**
  For example, Organic Food Growers Annual Conference, Omaha, Nebraska, July 12–14, 2000.

- **Why?**
  In the above example, the event may have provided an opportunity to see whether the supermarket chain you work for could expand their range of organic products.

- **Who?**
  List any new or renewed contacts, giving their full names, positions and brief details of what they said.

- **What?**
  Perhaps you think your organic produce should be more clearly labeled.

Information-only reports

Memos and budget reports fall into this category. Their main objective is to pass on information, and it's up to you to decide the most logical order in which to present it.

The order will usually be obvious: by department, product type, size, geographical area, age, etc. Occasionally, there will be no obvious, logical order. If this is the case, simply present the material in the way that is easiest for your reader to take in.

The research report

This is the most demanding type of report to write, since an important decision may rest on its findings. It usually involves a lot of information which must be presented in the most understandable way possible.

It needn't be long. In fact, a busy manager will be grateful for a report that can be read quickly and easily, but it must meet an objective as fully as possible. Your task is to sift out relevant from irrelevant information and present the facts clearly and concisely. You may also be asked to make recommendations based on the information contained in the report.

TYPE OF REPORT	POINTS TO BEAR IN MIND
Debriefing	How much does your audience already know about the subject? If you attended a new conference, tell them the background of it. Consider making recommendations, such as whether a delegate should be sent in future or whether your organization should have a booth at it.
Information Only	Don't ramble. This may not be the most glamorous of reports to write, but you won't score any points for providing irrelevant information.
Research	If this is the first time you've written a report of this kind, take a look at other examples that are well regarded. If you have a mentor, request help.

Planning a report

The most important part of report writing is the very beginning: knowing exactly what you will be writing about. If you set off with a clear statement of what the report is intended to achieve, every stage of the writing will be that much easier. If you're not really clear about your goal, you will waste time in gathering information, and your writing will lack confidence.

Setting a clear objective

The objective is a shorthand plan of the report you are about to write. It will guide you to the right sources of information and help you to decide which questions need to be answered. It must be as precise as possible.

Whoever asked you to write the report may have been rather general about what you were expected to do. Perhaps she said something like: "I was speaking to a client the other day, and they were telling me how terrific their new phone system is. Perhaps we should change to it. Can you look into it and get back to me with a report?"

Since you're the one writing the report, you need to be absolutely sure what is expected of you. Ideally, you should write down what you think your objective is and then show it to the person who has asked you to write the report. This ensures that you have understood what that person wants.

Producing a written objective also offers you an important safeguard. The person who commissioned the report may be unclear in their own mind about

PRODUCING A CLEAR OBJECTIVE
Once you've decided who your audience is, you can write down your objective. If the report is aimed at the marketing director, then the vague spoken objective:

"I was speaking to a client the other day and all she could talk about was her company's new phone system. Perhaps we should change to it."

could become something like:

"Investigate the pros and cons of changing the telephone system, so that it can more effectively handle requests from customers and keep them informed about new products."

what she has asked you to do. This vague idea may change between the time she commissioned the report and the moment you deliver it. No matter how good your report, if it's not what she thought she asked you for, she will be disappointed. And, since she is the boss, it will be difficult for you say: "But that's not what you asked me for."

Who are you writing for?

Determining who will read your report will help you to define your objective. The finance director may have asked for the report, but will the entire board of directors read it? Consider how the approach and content of the report will differ depending on the audience.

■ **Board of Directors**
Directors are likely to be interested in the strategic importance for the organization of a new telephone system. They will want your report to indicate whether the system would improve the organization's overall performance, although you would also have to include cost, marketing benefits and technical support.

■ **Chief Financial Official**
She will want to know about cost. How expensive is a new telephone system and will there be any long-term savings? Are there special deals for existing customers or different ways of paying?

■ **Marketing director**
She will want to know how the system could be used to improve service to customers. Perhaps sales are currently being lost because the phone isn't answered fast enough. Could a new system allow customers to leave a message rather than wait to speak to an operator?

■ **Information technology manager**
She will be interested in the systems the product uses and how it would tie in with existing products. What sort of technical support is offered, under what terms and for how long? Does the manufacturer have a good reputation?

■ **Human resources manager**
She will be interested in how a new telephone system will affect employees. Will there be job losses among receptionists? What sort of retraining will be necessary, and employeeswill it be provided in-house or contracted out? What is the best way of telling other employees about the new telephone system and how it can be used?

Ask yourself the following questions when assessing your readership:
■ How much do they know already about the subject?
■ How much do they need to know?
■ What don't they need to know?

Carrying out research

Don't begin your research before you've made a plan for organizing your research and findings. If you do, you're in danger of becoming swamped by facts and figures, or of wasting hours chasing information that's not relevant to your report.

Your research plan

You may already have developed a way of arranging material that suits you. If not, try the approach outlined below. Its advantage is that it makes you think about the questions your readers will have in mind as they start to look at your report.

1 Write down your objective

"Investigate the pros and cons of changing the telephone system so that it can deal with requests from customers and keep them informed about new products."

2 Divide the objective into questions that need to be answered

For example, your main questions might include:

■ What system do we have at the moment?
■ How do customers now ask for information?
■ How do we tell customers about new products?

■ What are the main new telephone systems on the market that could help customers?
■ What specific features are we looking for in a new system?

3 Add supplementary questions if necessary

Under some of your main questions, you might want to ask additional questions. For example, under the main question "What system do we have at the moment", you could ask:

■ How old is it?
■ What do receptionists like and dislike about it?
■ What do customers like and dislike about it?

4 Use the questions to order information as you find it

As you assemble your information, you will be able to slot a reference that will tell you where to find the answer into each of the sections. For example, under the main question "What are the main new telephone systems on the market that could help customers?" you might insert:

(a) *Telephony Weekly*, Oct. 2000, p.7
(b) Manufacturers' sales brochures and annual reports
(c) Financial analysts' report on the telecommunications market.

Sources of information

Talking to people

This could include customers, suppliers, people employed by your organization, or experts in a particular field. If your report is commercially sensitive, however, it may not be wise to discuss it with other people.

Be careful how you phrase your questions. "We're looking at ways of improving the telephone system" will receive a calmer and more constructive response from the receptionists than "We're thinking of scrapping the telephone system."

Asking questions that can't be answered with "yes" or "no" will give you more information: "What's bad about the telephone system?" rather than: "Do you like using the telephone system?"

Internal written sources

- Sales figures
- Brochures or letters sent to customers
- Internal publications
- Other reports, minutes of meetings, or proposals

External written sources

- Libraries – especially special or business libraries. Look for special reports; trade directories; market research; newspaper, magazine and trade press clippings; and reports by investment analysts.
- Trade organizations or chambers of commerce
- Government publications and statistics
- Government agencies designed to help businesses
- Publications by competitors or organizations in the field you're looking at, e.g. annual reports, catalogues, sales material, product launches

If you can't photocopy a document or type your comments straight into a computer, read back your notes as soon as you've made them to make sure they make sense.

TIMETABLE FOR RESEARCH

Don't leave long gaps of time between your periods of research, or you will have to reacquaint yourself with the information every time you go back to it. The fTollowing would be a good research schedule:

1. Brainstorm with someone, and make your research plan.
2. Set yourself a deadline, and draw up a timetable.
3. Pick a source that will give you a good start – perhaps a local business library – and set aside a morning or a full day to gather information there.
4. Identify information that might be hard to come by, and send off early requests for it.
5. Gather any information from within your organization.
6. Talk to people who might be able to help you fill in gaps in your knowledge or draw a conclusion.
7. Make a final effort to find information that has so far eluded you, but don't be tempted to exceed your deadline.

Putting a report together

You'll be far better off if you can start planning your report armed with more information than you need. But be ruthless and discard any information that isn't strictly relevant, however hard you have worked to obtain it.

Organizing your information

The body of your report will probably fall into four basic sections:

- present position/introduction (puts the report into context)
- problem (usually why the report is being written)
- possible strategy/options
- proposal/recommendations

You need to decide where each piece of information fits into this structure. Assemble all of the information you have gathered. Go through each item, and make a note of the main point you want to include and the source. You can proceed in one of four ways:

- Jot down each finding on a large piece of paper.
- Add each reference to your research plan or mind map (see opposite).
- Write each item on a separate piece of paper, and divide them into groups or headings.
- Write out the four basic section headings given above, and put each finding under one of them

MAKE IT EASY ON THE EYE
Keep the layout simple and straightforward. You're not trying to win a design award, so avoid using all the fancy fonts (two are quite enough) and random icons your computer can offer.

- Use double spacing and wide margins.
- Include plenty of headings; they help break up the text, provide useful "signposts," and make it easier for the reader to refer back and forth if necessary. Don't use humorous headlines; opt for headings that are straightforward and immediately understood.
- Use lists or bullet points where appropriate; they are easier to read than blocks of text.
- Number the pages. You might also want to break up the text into numbered sections, which make it easier for the report to be discussed after everyone has read it.
- If you're using illustrations, make sure they're placed as near as possible to the related piece of text.

If you don't feel ready to move straight to the fourth option, any of the first three will allow you to review the information you've accumulated.

Structuring a formal report

Your organization will probably have a format for you to follow. Otherwise, use this structure as a guideline:

- Title page (Include your name, position, the date, and the degree of confidentiality.)
- Contents page
- Summary (This should consist of a few paragraphs summing up the main body of the report.)
- Terms of reference (Outline who asked you to write the report and any stipulations made about what it should contain.)
- Acknowledgments
- Objective
- Report
- Bibliography and sources (Include comments from individuals, as well as any published material.)
- Appendices (These can include information, such as survey results, graphs, charts, and case studies that are too long to go into the main body of the text but are referred to in the report.)
- Glossary

Writing the report

Perhaps the hardest part of writing a report is putting that first sentence down on paper. But if you've spent enough time planning the report and you have a clear idea of its structure, the writing should come easily.

After weeks of research, you may feel like an expert in the subject; but don't resort to jargon. And if you don't quite understand something, leave it out; or find out what it means. Don't risk undermining a well-researched report because of a moment of laziness.

CREATING A MIND MAP

A mind map is a bit like brainstorming by yourself and on paper: put your brain into free-fall and see what it comes up with. The idea is to generate plenty of ideas without worrying too much about structuring your thoughts. Instead of making lists, just jot down words or phrases as they occur to you, using arrows to show how one thought leads to another.

So, if you're thinking about a new telephone system you might first think about what is good and bad about the old system. Under the heading "Old" you might have a line leading to another heading, "bad" with connected thoughts such as "slow", "keeps customer waiting", "doesn't provide information".

A second line, leading to a heading "good", might have thoughts such as "personal", "familiar" and "interactive".

6

Developing a customer profile
The direct approach
Writing to sell
Giving clear directions

Who is your customer?
How can you reach the customer?
Are you going over your reader's head?

Writing for the customer

We've already looked closely at the most common way of communicating with your customer – by letter or e-mail. But there are countless, more subtle ways in which you will write to or for your customer. Often, you will know very little about that customer. You may even have to write for potential rather than actual customers. Writing for an unknown reader requires care and imagination.

Objectives

Your communication will usually be prompted by one of two motives: to convey information to them or to gather feedback from them. Both will be vital to your business.

Conveying information can include telling customers how your product works. Asking for feedback could involve carrying out market research about the service or product you offer and how either could be improved. Market research can range from the highly sophisticated – and highly expensive – work carried out by organizations who specialize in this area, to a simple letter sent out to a customer. Either way, the results are a useful sales management tool.

Who's out there?

The most basic question is: "Who is my customer?" Finding the answer needn't be difficult or expensive. You could, for example, print a few questions on the back of your invoices. Remember to keep them short and straightforward: "Where did you hear of the company?", "What product ranges do you buy?", or "How do you rate our service?"

Producing a questionnaire

Sending out a detailed direct-mail survey takes money and thought, if you are to get a good response that provides the information you need. You should be sure of exactly what you want to use the information for. To get the best possible response, you will need to consider the factors discussed below.

Questions

Layout must be clear and leave plenty of room for answers. Start with a straightforward question that will encourage the customer to respond and continue. Questions must be unambiguous and follow a logical order.

Length

Be ruthless with the number of questions you pose. A smaller number is more likely to be answered, although this depends partly on how you present them.

Interest

If you can "connect" with your reader, he or she will be more likely to answer your questions. For example, a cat owner is more likely to respond to a questionnaire about toys for pets, which someone who owns a sports car will be more interested in telling you what he likes about high-performance cars.

Incentives

This could be a free gift, entry into a raffle or a discount coupon. Or you could write a compelling cover letter saying why the findings matter: to help medical research or improve an existing service. If you're writing to a business, offer a copy of the findings.

Convenience

Make it easy for the reader to reply. Include a stamped, addressed envelope, or print questions on the back of a pre-paid postcard.

Confidentiality

Some people will only take part if they can remain anonymous or are certain that their details will be kept private. Others, particularly business people, are not so shy. Make sure they know that their privacy will be respected.

Timing

Avoid sending out your mailing at a time of year when many people are likely to be on vacation or around Christmas, when your request might get lost in the seasonal mail. Some of your customers might have busy times of year. An accounts department will be particularly hectic near the end of the fiscal year; another customer might be attending an important trade fair.

The direct approach

Direct mail means sending a piece of advertising material – a brochure, leaflet or sales letter – directly to the customers at their offices or homes. It has several important advantages over other forms of advertising:

- It is a good way of reaching a well defined group of customers, especially if you have a long message to convey. The group of customers might be defined by their interests, where they live, or how much money they have.
- It is useful if your message relates to a particular date – if you're opening a new store or launching a new product, for example – because it can be timed for maximum impact.
- Its effectiveness is easy to measure. You will know exactly how many people replied to a partiuclar sales pitch and how many actually went on to buy the product or service.
- You can build on successful direct-mail operations to target customers who have bought from you in the past, for example, when a related product is being launched.

Sales letters

The sales letter is the cheapest form of direct-mail tool. Writing an effective sales letter uses all the writing skills we have already looked at, but take another look at "The persuasive letter" in the chapter on letter writing.

A sales letter will be longer than most other letters you write, but resist the temptation to ramble. The letter should include all the reasons why the product will improve the customer's life. It should also address any potential doubts they might have and tell them where they can buy your product.

The beginning

- If you don't know the name of the person to whom you are writing, use a title or other expression to make the letter more personal, i.e. "Dear Chocolate Lover," "Dear Grandparent," "Dear Librarian ...."
- Open with a paragraph that immediately grabs readers' attention by surprising them, making them think, or showing that you're on the same wavelength as they are. For example: "Did you know lettuce was once used as an antiperspirant? We're not suggesting you try this solution, but we know our new gardening hoe will take some of the sweat out of gardening ...", or "Does your partner's snoring keep you awake at night?" Make sure they can't resist reading on.

HOW EFFECTIVE ARE YOUR SALES LETTERS?

If you want to know whether you could improve on your sales letter, try experimenting with it. Introduce one small change: make the letter slightly longer or shorter, use sub-heads to introduce different points, or change the use of adjectives.

You could also consider reordering your arguments, making your approach emotional rather than practical, or changing the font you use or the size or quality of paper or envelope. Don't make too many changes, however; or it will not be possible to tell which, if any, affected the response.

Now, send out half the batch of letters without the change and half with the slightly different look. Once the responses are in, you will be able to gauge which version of the letter was the most effective.

Make your letter clear and approachable.
- If your letter runs to more than one page, write on only one side of the paper.
- The right side of the paragraphs should be ragged (as in this book), not justified; that is, each line doesn't end exactly below the one above. This makes the type look more friendly and less regimented.

Make it easy

Tell the reader exactly what they have to do to purchase your product or service – where to obtain it, how to fill in the coupon, which number to ring. Make it even more tempting by offering a discount if they purchase by a certain date or order a minimum amount.

First impressions

The very first contact the customer will have with your company may be when your letter arrives in their in box. Your "sales pitch" can start at this point, too.

Consider using an envelope that's an unusual shape, size or color, or has an interesting design. A letter to raise funds for a wildlife charity, for example, could portray a lion's yawning mouth.

Pose an interesting question to make a bold statement: "Why are women bad at parking?" The reader will have to open the envelope to discover that women aren't bad at parking, but that 90 percent of men think they are.

Producing a brochure

Brochures are a particular form of advertising; but, unlike advertising in a newspaper or magazine, a brochure allows you more space to convey your message, either through words or pictures. You can reproduce lavish photographs or highly technical drawings of your product, and include detailed information.

You can send the brochure to exactly the people you want to target. If your brochure is distributed as an insert in a magazine, you have less control over who might read it. Brochures are expensive to produce; and, if you want to reach a lot of people, it would be more economical to use a simple sales letter.

THE BROCHURE EXPERTS

The holiday industry produces some of the best brochures around – probably because a brochure plays a major part in helping people to choose a holiday. The most successful examples present pages of complicated information in an attractive way. They make you feel that they are written especially with you in mind: you deserve to be sitting on a beach sipping a tequila sunrise or hurtling down the best ski run in Europe.

When is a brochure appropriate?

Sometimes a sales letter is not adequate to market a product. The three important factors are the visual appeal of the product, cost, and luxury value.

■ **Visual appeal**
Do customers need to see the product? If they're buying nails or diapers, probably not. If they want a kitchen or vacation home, however, illustrations are essential.

■ **Cost**
If you're asking your readers to spend a lot of money, they will want to see substantial information on the product. Expensive products, such as private education or cars, usually require a brochure.

■ **Luxury**
The luxurious product demands a luxurious form of selling. A well-produced brochure will properly reflect the value of the product.

Making the product relevant

When you're writing a brochure, always think of how your product can make life more pleasant for your customer. Financial services, for example, can be tedious products to write about – and to read about – unless you take the leap of imagination that will relate them directly to your customer.

- A garage wanted to sell a warranty that guaranteed a car's cooling system and provided roadside assistance. Instead of talking about what makes a cooling system fail, it described being stuck in a traffic jam on a hot day with a car full of screaming children and the car's temperature gauge steadily climbing. Is 50 dollars a year too much to pay to avoid this nightmare, the brochure asked?

This brochure works well because, instead of going into the mechanics of the cooling system or the financial wisdom of a warranty, it relates directly to the customer in terms they can understand by painting a vivid picture of a stressful situation anyone would wish to avoid.

- A credit card company's brochure showed a football fan anxiously watching his team on television, a bridegroom calling the tow truck to get him to the church on time, a teenage girl chatting to her boyfriend on the phone, and a family cooking pasta – all thanks to the credit card. The brochure went on to describe how the card offered a warranty on the television set and discounts on membership of a

---

DON'T FORGET THE BASICS

When you're trying to make your brochures as appealing as possible, don't lose sight of the basic content. Be sure to include the following:

- contents page
- size, color, and different models of what you're selling
- where you can buy the product (if by mail order, include delivery charges and other costs)
- price list

Optional extras could include technical details, testimonials from satisfied customers, or a piece about your company and its history, if you think this will help to sell the product.

---

towing service, long-distance telephone calls, and fuel bills. Credit cards are intrinsically dull subjects. What makes them interesting is how they can improve our lives and allow us to have fun, and the brochure focuses on these benefits only. It also cleverly includes a range of potential customers – the football fan, the teenage girl, the young man about to be married, the family at home – for the widest possible appeal. Most people could relate to one of these groups, and each "story" is much more interesting than the financial service being sold.

Writing instructions

Anyone who has ever tried to put together a piece of furniture from a self-assembly kit will know just how annoying poorly written instructions can be. Or perhaps you've arrived late somewhere because the directions omitted a vital piece of information. By comparison, think how grateful you've been for good instructions. Perhaps you have stayed in a rented house that has clear instructions about how to use the central heating, stove and other gadgets. Or remember that Christmas when you saved the day by assembling a small child's new toy in time to stop a major tantrum?

Often, the trouble with poor instructions is that the writer knows too much. He has failed to put himself in the position of the person who is trying to operate a piece of machinery for the first time or who is unfamiliar with a part of town. The writer needs to take a step backwards mentally and imagine that he is doing something for the very first time.

Another problem is that the writer of the manual or set of instructions may know very little about the reader. Have they ever operated a fax machine before? Is this their first visit to a particular conference center, or to the town where it is located?

WRITING FOR JUAN IN BUENOS AIRES

Good instructions are written so that they make sense wherever the reader is – whether that's a position of complete ignorance or a degree of sophistication. A highly experienced writer who produces technical banking manuals says he finds it helps to dream up an imaginary reader to help him write in plain English. For him that person is Juan in Buenos Aires. Juan has been in his banking job for just three weeks, and English is his third language.

Directions

■ Make sure you mention landmarks that the average person would notice, not things that are of particular interest only to you. A large hotel is a better bet than a small shop, for example.

■ Don't include movable landmarks. The construction work that has ruined the view from your office window for the past year may be finished the day your visitors are due.

■ Consider which form of transportation your reader will be using: car, taxi, underground train, railway, airport or foot. You may need to give different instructions depending on how they will arrive.

- If someone is arriving by car, make sure you include information about parking, one-way streets and roadwork. Include tips on how to get back on track if they take the wrong exit off the highway.
- If there is more than one entrance to a building, be sure to identify the right one for your visitor.
- Once you've directed your visitor safely to the building, decide whether they need help to get around the interior, too.
- Include information on access for disabled visitors.
- Try out the directions yourself; or, better still, give them to a friend who doesn't know the area.

Instructions

- Lengthy instructions should have a contents page.
- Outline any precautions that should be taken, and explain why.
- List all materials and equipment needed so that the reader doesn't discover half way through assembly that a vital piece is missing.
- Advise how easy and difficult various stages are, so that readers can pace themselves or call in help if necessary.
- Consider dividing instructions into sections such as "installation," "getting started," and "special features," so readers can immediately identify the section most relevant to them.
- Give the reader only as much information as he needs – no more and no less. Providing too much detail can be as confusing as not giving enough.
- Be as precise as you can about the terms you use. Is the device that turns the machine on a switch, a knob, or a lever? Using the wrong word can leave the reader searching for something that isn't there.
- If there are areas that can be confusing, point this out. For example, a fax machine might have two settings that are easily mixed up – one in which the red light flashes and another in which the same light flashes even faster.

7

Raise your profile
Address the lay reader
Reach a wider audience
Get published

Who's out there?
How can you reach them?
What do they want to read?

Know your media

Getting your name or that of your organization in the press is one of the cheapest and most effective forms of advertising. An article about you, or in which you are mentioned, will give you greater credibility than many expensive advertising campaigns.

Who's out there?

Don't limit yourself to the most obvious publications. There are plenty of others that may be interested in your story.

- Newspapers – dailies, weeklies, free, and subscription, national, local and regional
- Magazines
- Trade publications – covering your own industry or an industry that might be interested in your press release
- Radio – local and national
- Television – local and national, cable and satellite, news and feature programs.
- Internet – special websites.

BUILDING UP THE PICTURE

Treat journalists like any other reader; find out as much about them and the organization they work for as possible. Read their publications or watch or listen to their shows, then build up a comprehensive profile. Make a note of the following information, most of which will apply to all forms of media.

- How often and when it appears
- How many editions it prints and whether there are local editions
- Cover price
- Circulation and geographical coverage
- Any regular sections or supplements, when they appear, their deadlines and who's in charge of each
- Key editorial people: editor, news editor, features editor, supplements editor, specialist reporters
- Any personal contacts
- Freelance journalists
- Whether the publication/show is running a campaign
- Profile of typical reader/listener/viewer: age, income, where they live, political leanings, and interests. The kind of advertising carried will give you some clues to this.

Writing a press release

The constant demand for news means that journalists are always on the lookout for an interesting press release that can help them fill a few column inches or that they can build into a longer article. But don't let this insatiable demand make you complacent. If your press release is difficult to understand, doesn't seem relevant to the journalist's market, or is just plain dull, it will follow a fast track to the trash basket.

Think like a journalist

Journalists are taught to ask themselves whether a potential story passes the "So what?" test. In other words, if they told someone about the story, would that person be interested or would her reaction be, "So what?"

If your press release fails to pass the test, try presenting the information in a different way. Compare these two headlines at the top of a press release:
- "Bio-idea Inc. launches new anti-coagulant product"
- "Blood product could save 300 children's lives a year"

Saving lives is newsworthy; an anonymous technical product is not. Try to think of your story in as personal terms as possible. If you were telling it to a small child, how would you capture his interest?

Give your story a spin

To make your story relevant to a general market, you may need to think of an angle that will catch people's interest.

- **Charity**
  Charitable events are popular with the local press and show your organization in a favorable light.

- **"Topsy-turvy" stories**
  Are you selling wine to France or employing prison inmates to make burglar alarm systems?

- **The populist spin**
  You've solved a complex problem in physics and, at the same time, another puzzle – the best way to tie a necktie.

- **Silly stories**
  You've launched a sophisticated new range of bedding but all news editors care about is that the design makes it easy to change a duvet cover.

- **Big names**
  Is there someone famous who uses your product or has praised it?

- **Record-breaking**
  You've just opened the first fish and chip shop in Russia, or sold the millionth clock radio.

Any inaccuracies in a press release could haunt you for a long time. Even if the journalist throws the press release away after using it, the story they write will become a permanent record for others to refer to. If it contains wrong information, there is a good chance that other journalists will perpetuate the errors. So, be sure to provide the correct information in the first place.

Writing a press release

Occasionally, your press release will be reprinted word for word. If it's too long, it will be cut from the bottom; so don't leave a vital fact until the last paragraph.

Write like a journalist

Build your press release like a pyramid, with the most important information at the very top and other facts supporting its structural base. No matter how many of the bottom layers are removed, the pyramid's shape will remain. Put this to the test with a news story; if it's well written, you should be able to tell what it's about from the first paragraph, or even the first line.

Ideally, the first sentence should answer the following questions: who, what, where, why, and when. "Ian Jameson will become vice-president of Superior Biscuits' overseas division, based in Dallas starting on May 1 2001 and will help spearhead the company's expansion into Eastern Europe."

Using quotes

Journalists like quotes, but make sure they're not bland. Always give the person's name, title, and organization. You don't have to use a company president. A satisfied customer or an expert in the field may be just as valid. Always explain why a person is being quoted. Has he been studying a subject for several years or does she belong to a respected organization?

Embargoes

There are two main reasons for using an embargo – that is, a request to the publication not to publish the information in the press release before a specified date.

First, if you're releasing something that is either very long or very complicated – a report or a set of statistics – an embargo gives journalists time to digest the release. Second, you might want to ensure that a particular publication gets to use the release before others do. An embargo will prevent other publications from stealing the exclusive. This technique can, of course, be used to exclude publications, but this is a dangerous game to play. If a paper thinks you are trying to stop it printing something, it may try to dig up a new angle that you had not bargained for.

Before using an embargo, ask yourself if you really need it. It can be tempting to add the word "embargo" to the top of a press release to make it sound more important. This won't fool journalists and is more likely to annoy them. Some may even break the embargo if they can't see any justification for it.

Photos

Including a photo will increase your chances of getting published.

- Send a color photo unless told otherwise. It can be reproduced in black and white or color as the publication prefers.
- Label the back of the photos with all the necessary information.
- Use interesting, close-up shots. Avoid pictures of people talking on the telephone.
- Don't use photos taken in photo booths. They are never flattering.

Don't feel you have to include every scrap of information in a press release. Leave some gaps so that the reporter is prompted to follow up the release with a phone call.

WHAT TO INCLUDE IN A PRESS RELEASE

- At the very top write your organization's name (or use corporate letterhead) and the words "press release."
- Write a headline to sum up the content, and make it punchy – ten words or fewer, if you can.
- Use 8½" x 11" paper, write only on one side, and double-space your text.
- Keep it short – around 500 words. If it covers more than one page, write "m/f" (more follows) or "more" in the bottom right-hand corner. After the final sentence, leave a few blank lines and then put "end" in the center of the page.
- At the bottom include the names, titles, and telephone numbers of people for the journalist to contact if they have questions. Include more than one person, make sure they will be available, or give days and times when they can be reached. It is irritating for a journalist to be told that a spokesperson is available only to find that he or she is not.
- Use "Notes to editors" at the end of the press release to provide background details without cluttering up the main body of the text. This might include information about the organization or the product.
- If it's not on your corporate letterhead, include other information, such as e-mail addresses and website details at the end of the press release.

Sample press release

WHERE TO PLACE THE STORY

■ Each of the local newspapers, radio, and TV stations in towns with a Palmtree Hotel.

■ Hotel, restaurant, and catering trade press.

■ Sports and general-interest magazines.

■ Sections: where to stay, eating out, cooking (Chase could give his favorite recipe), sports pages, profile section.

The following, fictitious press release is accompanied by a picture of a smiling Chase Gordon wearing a baseball shirt and tucking into a meal at a Palmtree Hotel. The press hit contains a brief biography of Chase and a map showing the locations of all Palmtree Hotels.

PRESS RELEASE
For Immediate Release

May 21 2000

Hotel Chain Appoints Ex-American Baseball Star to Improve its Menu

Palmtree Hotels has recruited Chase Gordon as a non-executive director to improve the quality and variety of its menu.

Chase, 49, played for the Boston Red Sox for 13 years before going on to pursue his passion for cooking. He attended the Louisiana Culinary School and owns a restaurant in Cape Cod.

Phil Scrivener, managing director of Palmtree Hotels, said: "Our new non-executive director combines business sense and culinary knowledge with a competitive desire to be the best."

Chase said: "As a professional baseball player, I discovered how important it is to stay in a hotel that makes you feel at home. Good food plays a vital part in making guests feel comfortable."

- end -

Phil Scrivener can be contacted at:
Chase Gordon is available today on:

Note to editors: Palmtree Hotels runs 150 small to medium sized hotels in towns and cities in the USA (see enclosed map). It was started in 1930 by a shoe millionaire who, when he was a travelling salesman, had found it difficult to find a decent place to stay.

Getting a feature published

Writing an article is one step better than simply producing a press release. You have greater, but not absolute, power over what appears in the magazine or newspaper, and writing the article will raise your profile.

Unless your organization is paying for an article to run in a newspaper or magazine, you will have to persuade the publication that you can write something their readers will enjoy. One way of doing this is to make the article timely.

Hooks

Editors look for "hooks" – a reason why the article is relevant now – on which to hang features. If you can think of a good hook, you have more chance of getting your feature published. Anniversaries, regular celebrations, timely news stories, and topical issues can all make good hooks.

Anniversaries

Be on the look-out for any event that you can link to your organization. A fertility clinic could run a feature based on the anniversary of the first test-tube baby, describing advances that have been made in fertility treatment and comparing the old procedures with new developments.

Regular celebrations

These could include Christmas, Chinese New Year, Saint Patrick's Day, and so on. For example, you could write a feature explaining what precautions your children should take on Halloween, and mention your company's range of candies.

One-offs

The area is hit by drought, and gardens start to suffer. You explain how gardeners can save water and how your organization's self-watering irrigation system can help.

Issues

Salmonella scares are rampant. As an egg producer, you tell customers how best to keep foods fresh.

If you're having trouble devising a "hook" for your story, try approaching a publication in the "silly season" – usually from July to September, when news is short and editors are desperate for copy. They still won't publish just anything, but they may be more willing to consider your story.

INCREASE YOUR CHANCES
Give editors what they need: an interesting piece written to required length and on time and, ideally, some good pictures to go with it.

- **Length:** If the article is too short, it won't be used; or you'll be asked to rewrite. If it's too long, it will be chopped, usually from the bottom.
- **Deadline:** If you miss it, the paper will have to find a replacement for your piece and won't commission you again.
- **Photos:** The editor will be delighted to have any suggestions. Follow the usual guidelines for sending in photos (see page 85).

Planning a readable feature

Once you've got the editor's acceptance you want people to actually read the feature. If you're writing an "advertorial," which means your organization pays for the feature to be included, you can be as boring as you like. If you're writing for the editorial pages, the feature will be changed dramatically or scrapped altogether, if it's dull. Either way, you and your company lose. Your priority must always be to interest your reader.

Now read on

Which articles from the last magazine or newspaper you read stick in your mind and why? Perhaps it was for one or more of the following reasons:

- You felt compelled by the opening paragraph to read on.
- The article was illustrated with a funny or powerful photograph or drawing.
- Someone famous was mentioned in the piece.
- The writer used memorable images.
- You could relate to the article.
- The subject interested you.
- The facts or examples used shocked or surprised you.
- The subject was so important that you felt you had to read the story.

WHAT DO PORK PIES AND SCULPTURES HAVE IN COMMON?
Your readers know nothing about your organization and they're not technical. You want your company to sound as interesting, funny, glamorous as possible. How do you do it? One way is to identify the parts of the business they can relate to and then, once you've secured their interest, gradually fill in the other information.

Take a company that makes sophisticated, high-pressured, injection-molding machinery. Most of the instruments are used for obscure industrial purposes, but some might be used for purposes that anyone can relate to. For example, one instrument might be used to clean difficult-to-reach parts of a complex sculpture in Central Park. Another might be used to inject the jelly into pork pies.

These are two aspects of the business you probably wouldn't feature in your company's annual report. But they provide strong images for the lay reader, who will probably always think of the company when they eat a pork pie.

Structuring a feature

Every feature has a beginning, middle, and end. This may sound simplistic, but using a straightforward structure will help you order your thoughts.

A startling beginning

The opening paragraph must grab the reader's attention. Suppose you work for the fictitious injection molding company mentioned on page 88 and you're writing a profile of the business. Compare these opening paragraphs:

1 "The fact that the Statue of Liberty has a clear view over Staton Island is due directly to Acme Injection Moldings. If it weren't for Acme, America's most famous lady would be squinting across the island through a mire of pigeons' droppings and ingrained New York dirt."

2 "Acme Injection Moldings, based in upstate New York, meets a range of industrial functions for customers around the world. It has been in existence for over 150 years and uses the latest of modern technology."

The first paragraph presents a vivid picture; the second tries to cram in too much information and does not engage the reader's attention.

The middle: bringing facts to life

Facts by themselves can be dull; this is especially true of statistics. Put them into context by comparing them to objects the reader can relate to.

Imagine you work for your local community government or an aluminium producer, and you want to encourage people to recycle their rubbish. The feature you write for the local newspaper must contain the necessary facts to support your case. But how do you present those facts?

"The average Chicago family fills its dustbins with 1,760 pounds of waste each year," is meaningless to most people. However, if you add that 1,760 pounds is more than the weight of a Chevrolet, your readers will have a strong graphic image of how much waste you're talking about.

You might go on to say that Americans throw away about seven billion soda cans a year. Of these, 60 percent are aluminium – the easiest to recycle. Again, these figures are meaningless unless you bring them to life. You could, for example, point out that if the aluminium empties were placed side by side they would circle the globe – six times. Suddenly, aluminium cans don't sound quite so dull. A picture of someone appearing to "drown" in cans will drive home the image.

Structuring a feature

End on an upbeat note

Finishing a feature can be as difficult as beginning, but don't simply trail off. End on a positive note, perhaps by looking to the future. If your feature has been talking about a problem, look at solutions that are being developed, as well as ones already in use.

Always give your name and title at the end of piece, preferably in italics. This is also the place to add any extra information for the reader to follow up: relevant phone numbers, publications, addresses of organizations, or websites. They don't need to be linked to your organization, but make it as easy as possible for the reader to contact you.

Trade publications

Use the above structure for a trade publication. But be careful not to talk down to your reader, who may understand the market better than the average person. They will probably want to know technical details. This information might be better separated from the main body of the text, perhaps in a separate box or "sidebar." Discuss this with the editor, who commissioned the piece.

QUESTIONS TO ASK YOURSELF ABOUT YOUR FEATURE

Would I read this feature? If not, is it because:
   (a) The illustrations are dull and don't attract my attention?
   (b) It isn't relevant to me, my family, or my buisness?
   (c) It lacks a sense of humor?

If it attracts my attention, would I read it to the very end? If not, is it because:
   (a) The style slows down after the first few paragraphs?
   (b) The writer doesn't continue to relate to me?
   (c) There's no new or startling information?

Would I remember the article after reading it? If so, is it because:
   (a) It made me laugh?
   (b) It includes some interesting facts?
   (c) It led me to discuss the subject with someone afterwards?

Writing ad copy

Ads are expensive, producing them requires creativity, and the end product has to reflect the vision of a team of people. If you're given the task of writing ad copy, you should enlist as much help as you can.

Make sure you know exactly what you want an ad to accomplish by drawing up a creative concept statement. It should include the following information.

- **The aim of the advertisement**
  Is it to increase sales, raise awareness of your organization, or launch a new product or service?

- **The target audience**
  Be as specific as possible about this (see Chapter Two).

- **Unique Selling Point (USP)**
  What sets your product or service apart from the competition? Is it the price, the materials used, or the organization's expertise?

- **Tone**
  What sort of approach will you use: aggressive, seductive, authoritative?

- **Proposed media**
  Where do you intend to run the ad?

The headline

Your ad will be jostling for attention with several others. The headline must reach out and grab your readers. After that, it needs to persuade them to buy the product or service.

The headline must be immediately understood. Few readers will be bothered to spend time trying to figure out a convoluted pun. Straightforward headlines are usually the most effective, as in these examples.

- "Freshness at your fingertips." (Deodorant)
- "Taste and goodness in one small pot." (Yogurt)
- "Reliability teamed with style." (Computer)

The body copy

Keep the main message short. Unless someone is particularly interested in what you are selling, they are unlikely to read much of your advertisement.

- "Don't read this book if you want a good night's sleep. From the first gripping sentence to the startling conclusion, you won't be able to stop reading Donald Webster's new thriller. Are you up to the challenge?"

Imagine you are chatting with a friend. Use simple language and break up the main points into paragraphs or by using illustrations.

Don't forget to include the essentials in your advertising copy: your company, name, and telephone number. You might want to include a list of stockists or a coupon and an illustration.

Recruitment advertising

Recruitment advertising is expensive, so make the best use of it with a carefully worded message that will attract the maximum number of eligible candidates.

What to include
Be sure to mention everything the potential candidate needs to know:
- position
- brief description of role
- salary and other perks
- reporting structure
- company name, location, and industry
- qualifications and experience required

- how to apply and closing date

If you're using a recruitment agency, reassure the applicant that their personal information won't be sent to their own employer.

Style
Keep your writing crisp and interesting. After all, you're selling your organization and a job. Since space is limited you can use some jargon, especially if you are advertising for someone who knows your industry well. Lay out the advertisement exactly as you want it to appear in the newspaper or magazine. Specify any logos or style of lettering you want.

The Reel Thing film production house is looking for a
GROUP FINANCIAL CONTROLLER

The successful candidate will help to guide this young company through the exciting next stage of its development. He or she will report directly to the chairman.

The position requires a computer-literate, qualified accountant. Experience in the movie industry and working overseas would be an advantage.

Salary range $55,000-$70,000

For further details send an 9" x 12" stamped, self-addressed envelope to:
Gillian Jones, The Reel Thing, 12 Industrial Estates, Los Angeles, CA.
Closing date for applications is May 8.

Develop your business writing skills

The skills you've learned in this book will help you improve your writing technique in your professional and personal life. This won't happen immediately; you will need practice to perfect your new skills. But you will be rewarded by increased efficiency, more confidence in written communications, and new opportunities to make a good impression on management and others.

Analyse your style

If you haven't already done so, use the questionnaire on pages 16–17 to help you identify areas in your writing style that need work. Do the questionnaire from time to time to see where you have improved.

Keep it simple

No matter how complex the subject you are tackling, don't forget the basics. Remember the four Ss and RAMP (see page 31). Every so often, check your fog index (see page 21).

Learn by example

Improve your technique by becoming a more critical reader. Analyze what you have read, whether it's the latest novel, a theater program, or a billboard. Why did you enjoy reading it, what didn't you understand, and why did certain images stay in your mind long after you read it.

Look at different kinds of business writing – pieces that fail and pieces that work well. Which of the fours Ss does a badly written piece not observe? What other rules does it break? Does a well written piece simply follow the rules? Does it use particular effects, such as an arresting visual image or off-beat approach to create its impact?

Write, write, write

Seek out opportunities to write. Something where you will have the time to spend on rewriting and polishing your style is ideal – perhaps a piece for your company's newsletter or an organization that you belong to.

Remember that good writing is as much about what you leave out as what you put in.

Soon writing will seem as natural to you as any other communication skill – like talking or smiling.

Index

If you liked Business Writing, by Midge Gillies check out these other great career-building books from AMACOM.

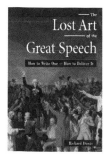

The Lost Art of the Great Speech
Richard Dowis

The authoritative speech-writing guide covers every essential element of a great speech, including outlining and organizing, beginning with a bang, making use of action verbs and vivid nouns, and handling questions from the audience. Plus, the book includes excerpts from some of history's most memorable speeches—eloquent words to contemplate and emulate.

$14.95 Order #7054-XBKM ISBN: 0-8144-7054-8

On the Art of Writing Copy, Second Edition
Herschell Gordon Lewis

One of the great copywriting artists of our day supplies 100 simple and time-tested rules anyone can implement to create powerful, effective copy. The book shows you how to adapt copy for each medium, including the Internet, and offers specific rules for direct mail letters, television, radio, online, fund raising, special interest groups, print ads, card decks. catalogs, and more.

$21.95 Order #7031-XBKM ISBN: 0-8144-7031-9

The Ultimate Book of Business Quotations
Stuart Crainer

Need to spice up a memo, add focus to a presentation, or simply have something unique to say at your next business lunch? This book has the solution. Filled with intriguing comments from thinkers in all walks of life, it is an unconventional compendium of quips, quotes, and sayings that are prefect for use by business people.

$24.95 Order # 0447-XBKM ISBN: 0-8144-0447-2

Plain Style
Techniques for Simple, Concise, Emphatic Business Writing
Richard Lauchman

This incisive guide suggests ways to think about writing—what it should look and sound like, as well as what it should accomplish—that can simplify how you choose to express your ideas. It offers 35 practical techniques that foster simplicity, conciseness, and emphasis.

$15.95 Order #7852-XBKM ISBN: 0-8144-7852-2

Call 1-800-262-9699 or order in your local bookstore.